HAINTS, WITCHES, AND BOOGERS
Tales from Upper East Tennessee

HAINTS, WITCHES, AND BOOGERS
Tales from Upper East Tennessee

by
Charles Edwin Price
Foreword by Richard Blaustein

John F. Blair, Publisher
Winston-Salem, North Carolina

Copyright © 1992 by John F. Blair, Publisher
Printed in the United States of America
All Rights Reserved

Second Printing, 1995

Printed on acid-free paper

Printed and bound by R. R. Donnelly & Sons
Book Design by Debra L. Hampton

Library of Congress Cataloging-in-Publication Data
Price, Charles Edwin, 1941–
    Haints, witches, and boogers : tales from Upper East Tennessee /
by Charles Edwin Price ; foreword by Richard Blaustein.
        p.   cm.
    ISBN 0-89587-093-2 :
    1. Ghosts—Tennessee. 2. Witchcraft—Tennessee. 3. Ghost
stories, American—Tennessee. I. Title.
BF1472.U6P75 1992
133.1'09768'9—dc20
92-12664

For
Linda Carmichel

CONTENTS

FOREWORD

Belief in ghosts, witches, and demons may be as old as the human capacity to symbolize. From the time of the Neanderthal cave dwellers to our own, belief in the existence of the soul, or some spiritual identity that survives physical death, has been found in virtually all human societies, along with credence in the powers of evil-minded people who bring harm to others through the manipulation of supernaturally charged symbols and communication with malign spiritual beings.

Why do most people believe in the supernatural? Is it because belief in a world beyond our own is more emotionally comforting than the prospect of total extinction and oblivion? Or is there actually a supernatural reality that exists independently of our personal beliefs and disbeliefs, an opaque reality that becomes transparent when the boundaries that normally separate the realms of the living and the dead are blurred?

Personally, I would rather let theologians and parapsychologists search for definitive answers to these questions. I am comfortable with the idea that witches, ghosts, and demons are real to the extent that we invest significance and power in them. By that relativistic standard, supernatural beings and forces are still real to many people in the modern world, including those who make their home in the hills and hollows of upper East Tennessee.

As interesting as these questions about the supernatural may be, what really fascinates me as a folklorist is the recurrence of widely distributed scenarios and themes—tale types and motifs, as folklorists prefer to call them—which cross cultural and linguistic boundaries. "The lady in white," "the vanishing hitchhiker," and "the revenant in animal form" are just a few of the motifs that have cropped up once again in this collection of supernatural tales gathered by Ed Price in upper East Tennessee.

Some of the tales in this book are nearly verbatim accounts of firsthand encounters with ghosts, witches, and demons drawn from taped interviews. Others are skillful retellings that illustrate the author's abilities as a journalist and narrative writer. And one report of a poltergeist is taken from a nineteenth-century newspaper account published in Jonesborough. As I have sifted through these tales, I have been struck by the fact that few, if any, of the motifs included within them are unique. Why is this?

Encounters with the supernatural are not random, chaotic experiences. The supernatural world, like the natural world, is governed by laws that can be expressed in the form of logical propositions. Ed Price and I have talked about "ghost logic," a concept based on the observation that all ghosts appear to be attached to particular places, objects, persons, or events in our world. These restless spirits seem to be suffering from a form of supernatural distress equivalent to neurosis or obsession, as though some powerful emotional trauma has caused them to become fixated upon a given focal point. Some ghosts are capable of direct interaction with the living; these spirits may be either malevolent or benevolent. Other ghosts manifest themselves to the living but appear to be unconscious of, or unable to, communicate with their audience, at least not directly. Nearly all of the ghost tales in this collection can be grouped into one or another of these categories.

Regardless of whether we believe in their existence, ghosts, like witches and demons, are part of our cultural lexicon and inventory.

This collection contains several humorous stories that play upon fear of ghosts, including two separate accounts of pranksters who disguise themselves as ghosts to frighten others, only to scare themselves. This is a commonly encountered motif. Here, too, we can see a compelling logic that leads to predictable consequences.

There is a logic in witchcraft as well. In our culture, witches receive supernatural powers from Satan in return for their souls. In most societies, witches are believed to be jealous, dangerous, antisocial individuals who inflict harm on others through magical means. Indeed, witches reveal themselves through manifestations of magical power that defy or transcend natural law. As the stories about witches in this collection clearly demonstrate, there are still people living in upper East Tennessee who believe in witches and, more to the point, others who are themselves believed to be witches.

This does not mean that upper East Tennesseans are particularly superstitious or backward, but rather that the supernatural in all of its godly and ungodly manifestations is very real to many people living today, just as it was to their ancestors. These traditions can be found in big cities as well as remote rural areas. A few years ago while attending the annual meeting of the American Folklore Society in Baltimore, I found myself wandering down a little street lined from end to end with shops specializing in dream books, magical herbs, potions, and candles. Magic and witchcraft were obviously alive to the customers of those stores.

Ed Price combines contagious enthusiasm for his subject with a vivid, uncluttered prose style. I wish there were more writers like him. I hope you enjoy reading this book as much as I enjoyed watching him put it together.

Richard Blaustein
Director of the Center for
Appalachian Studies and Services
East Tennessee State University

PREFACE

Somewhere in the shadows of East Tennessee State University's Burleson Hall lurks the moaning spirit of a distinguished academician who, decades ago, put a bullet through her brain.

In Kingsport, near the famous Netherland Inn, the specter of a man killed a half-century ago directs traffic over a dangerous road when thick fog shrouds the old waterfront.

In Hampton, there is a legend about a woman with no identity who, like Mary Poppins, mysteriously arrived with the wind one stormy night over a century ago.

Somewhere in Carter County, a farmer still lives in mortal fear, his life and livelihood dependent upon the "good will" of a horribly vindictive witch.

Upper East Tennessee has more than its share of haints, witches, and boogers. The terms *haints* and *boogers* are colloquialisms for ghosts and other supernatural beings. They are used chiefly by older folks. Upper East Tennesseans are neither fearful of nor cowed by the supernatural. Most natives heard ghost stories while they were still in swaddling clothes. The words *haint* and *booger* are more a reflection of an attitude toward the supernatural than a description of a frightening enigma. Perhaps this is so because native upper East Tennesseans are a rugged people. It took a rugged people to settle this isolated land in the first place.

Upper East Tennessee is located in a deep natural bowl, rimmed by the Unaka Mountains to the east and the Cumberland Plateau to the west. In the early years of settlement, the valley was virtually isolated by these natural barriers. The Unaka Mountains are especially steep, wild, and thickly forested. Some peaks in the range are among the highest east of the Rocky Mountains, and some of the passes through them are among the most difficult to traverse in North America.

Settling along the fertile banks of the Holston and Nolichucky rivers, early residents relied on cunning and industry to survive. For many years, new settlers came across the mountains in a mere trickle. Others entered this wildest of frontiers from the north, traveling down the Shenandoah Valley from Virginia and Pennsylvania. The initial settlers were people of Scotch-Irish, English, and German blood, with a smattering of French Huguenots sprinkled in.

With the coming of the railroads in the 1840s, upper East Tennessee cast aside its isolation. Immigrants flooded in via the shiny, winding ribbons of steel, built the cities of Johnson City, Kingsport, and Bristol, and established businesses and factories. The area boomed. The six counties of upper East Tennessee—Sullivan, Washington, Greene, Carter, Unicoi, and Johnson—welcomed outsiders. Not only were there plentiful jobs, but there were thousands of acres of unspoiled wilderness to enjoy.

Each city developed an economic personality. Kingsport, built around sprawling Tennessee Eastman, became an industrial town. Lacking large factories, Johnson City depended on services for its economy; within its city limits, there are four major hospitals and a medical school. Bristol attracted the railroads and became a commerce center.

Colleges and universities sprang up to educate upper East Tennessee's new citizens. As enrollments grew and upper East Tennesseans became better educated and more sophisticated, reliance on age-old folktales decreased—as did belief in ghosts.

Ghosts are creatures of the twilight. Apparitions emerge from the sunless hollows of the mind, glide from the corner of the eye, flit about in the dusky half-light of a forgotten structure or in the damp shade of a brier-tangled thicket. The sun disappears below the horizon and murky half-shadows appear. Even the sophisticated twentieth-century citizen becomes apprehensive at the approach of an all-encompassing darkness that cannot be controlled and that still holds unknown terrors. As Roger Bacon once said, superstitions, like bats, fly best at twilight.

A technologically based society tends to dismiss events it cannot explain without the aid of a computer printout, science, or logic, but belief in ghosts and the supernatural is more common than most people would like to think. According to a 1987 Epcot poll, 13 percent of Americans claim to have seen a ghost and one-third say they believe in ghosts. A national survey conducted by the University of Chicago's National Opinion Research Center reported that 42 percent of all Americans said they have been in contact with someone who has died. Among widows and widowers, the rate increased by two-thirds.

This collection of ghost tales from upper East Tennessee spans the gamut of the supernatural: troublesome poltergeists, malevolent apparitions, magical animals, evil witches, devils in the form of black dogs, ghostly figures in the fog, helpful spirits, vengeful spirits, protective spirits, fetching spirits, ghostly objects, and ghost lights. Most of these yarns were told to me orally, thereby placing them in the classic definition of folklore—stories passed along without benefit of the written word. A few tales in this book were assembled from a number of different sources because of their notoriety or because different people knew only a fragment of the complete story. And one story was taken from the yellowing pages of a nineteenth-century weekly newspaper.

The stories in this collection came from informants in all walks of life and from all educational and economic backgrounds. Storytellers included university professors, students, blue-collar workers, policemen, business people, retirees, farmers, American Indians, laborers, professionals, and even street people. The youngest informant was fourteen, the oldest ninety-seven. Folklore knows no boundaries of age or social status.

The real importance of the stories in this book is not in their entertainment value or their agelessness. The importance lies in their reflection of past and present beliefs, lives, and lifestyles—who we are and what we are in upper East Tennessee. We are members of a fraternity that reaches back hundreds of years, born in virgin forests, nursed on verdant mountainsides, and ready to embark on any exciting journey when the opportunity presents itself.

ACKNOWLEDGMENTS

I would like to thank Dr. Richard Blaustein, director of the Center for Appalachian Studies and Services at East Tennessee State University, for his inestimable help in assembling the list of motifs at the end of each story. He obtained these from Ernest W. Baughman's *Type and Motif Index of the Folktales of England and North America*, a standard guide utilized by folklorists to match recognized plot motifs from one folk story with those from another. Throughout the writing of this book, Richard also read and reread each of the stories, offering helpful tips and advice. Without his enthusiastic help, this book could not have reached its final form.

I offer a very special thanks to Linda Carmichel, assistant professor of English at ETSU, for reading and rereading my manuscript, for pointing out the many flaws in my prose, and for giving special encouragement. I imagine she must have gotten a bit weary each morning of treading on the scattered manuscript pages that I had shoved under her office door in the middle of the night.

I would like to thank Dr. Nancy Acuff of East Tennessee State University, a person well-acquainted with area ghost tales, for helping with the story of the Rotherwood ghosts, as well as for providing invaluable background information for the Netherland Inn ghost tale and the chapter on Lena Jones. Nearly ten years ago, Nancy helped me with a couple of documentary radio shows for WETS-FM, and these stories were part of the shows.

There is another person I cannot, under any circumstances, forget—Dr. Anne LeCroy, professor of English at ETSU. Anne is one of those very special people every writer needs on his side, someone whose infectious enthusiasm can cut through the worst case of writer's *block n' gloom*. Occasionally prodding me with home-made baked goodies, words of encouragement, and her marvelous conversation, Anne has always been—and will continue to be—one of my main sources of inspiration and assurance.

Finally, I would like to offer a special note of appreciation to folklorist Thomas Burton, professor of English at ETSU, who first suggested I assemble part of my collection of Appalachian ghost lore into a book. In the 1960s and 1970s, he and Professor Ambrose Manning collected thousands of songs and stories from upper East Tennessee and western North Carolina, especially from the Beech Mountain area. The Burton-Manning Collection of folklore, housed at the Archives of Appalachia at ETSU, is perhaps one of the finest collections of its type in the East. Especially in the realm of folk music, the Burton-Manning Collection stands as a monument to the dedication of two men bound and determined that southern Appalachian tradition should be set down and preserved for generations to come.

HAINTS, WITCHES, AND BOOGERS
Tales from Upper East Tennessee

THE
HAUNTED
CAVE

A tiny cave located on the Tipton-Haynes Farm near Johnson City is said to be a hotbed of supernatural activity, especially during the summer months. Misty visions centuries old appear—sights woven from ethereal plasma and repeated over and over like videotape recordings. The visions are tableaus of Indians and white men in buckskin—a three-dimensional parade of past events, much like an outdoor drama.

During the daytime, there is nothing sinister about the cave, but after dark, strange sights and sounds sometimes occur around its mouth. Legend says that at night, a ghostly campfire can be seen. Gathered around it are the shadowy forms of men laughing and eating their evening meal.

One witness saw a man dressed in buckskin who appeared to be stoking the fire. It could have been the ghost of Daniel Boone himself, but many lesser-known white hunters also used the cave at one time or another. As the witness crept closer for a better look, his foot snapped a twig, and the entire tableau faded into blackness. Seconds afterward, when he reached the entrance, he could swear that the aroma of burnt wood still hung in the air.

On another occasion, an eyewitness described a group of Indians at the entrance of the cave. He watched as one Indian, a slight and aged fellow, perhaps a chief, stood and began addressing the group. Although the apparition's mouth moved, no sound emerged. As he spoke, the others seemed to murmur to themselves and shake their heads. The old Indian was obviously trying to reason with his audience, but his listeners did not behave as if they agreed with what he was saying. The apparition lasted several minutes, then faded.

The sightings have been reported for years. There is, for example, a well-known story concerning a man named Robert McCormick, who decided to camp at the cave one night with his young son. After passing a pleasant evening chatting and eating their meal beside the campfire, father and son bedded down for the night. Since the July sky was clear and there was no threat of rain, they spread their bedrolls at the mouth of the cave.

About two o'clock in the morning, both were awakened by the sound of voices. Robert McCormick opened his eyes and was startled to find himself surrounded by a party of Indians. Thinking his friends were playing a practical joke, he called for the "Indians" to disperse and allow him some sleep. When there was no reply, he called out again, and the Indians suddenly faded into the darkness.

Stricken with terror, McCormick's son began screaming hysterically. He scrambled out of his bedroll and raced up the hill away from the cave, his equally panicked father close behind. Upon reaching the top, the son tripped and fell, allowing the father to catch up to him. Then McCormick glanced in the direction of the cave. The entrance was dark and no one was in sight. As he tried to quiet his son and keep himself under control, he could swear that somewhere down in the little valley he could hear the faint sound of laughter.

Robert McCormick's vision of the Indians was too elaborate to have been faked. Real men could not have vanished from view like that, and so suddenly. As the laughter faded from the valley, McCormick could not help but think that ghosts, like the living, must have a well-tuned sense of humor.

With as much history as the little cave has seen, it is not surprising that it should be the site of ghostly activity. For centuries, it was used as an overnight campsite by Indians and white explorers alike. In fact, anthropologists believe Neolithic Indians probably used the cave as early as 12,000 B.C. In the flickering light of campfires, weary men rested and told stories of their exploits and planned the next day's hunt or exploration.

The cave has hosted more than its share of distinguished visitors, including the first known white men to enter the region—James Needham and an indentured servant named Gabriel Arthur, both Englishmen. Their ghosts are said to be among those that haunt the cave.

As agents for Colonel Abraham Wood, the owner of a flourishing trading post in Virginia, Needham and Arthur were sent in 1673 to explore the wilderness south and west of the Appalachian Mountains and establish direct trade with Tomahitan Indian villages. Accompanying them were eight Tomahitan guides and an unsavory Occaneechee guide called Indian John. In his previous trading with Indians, Colonel Wood had been forced to employ members of the Occaneechee tribe as middlemen. The Occaneechee had managed to turn a good profit in reselling Indian goods to Colonel Wood, so they weren't eager to have Needham and Arthur establish direct ties with Indian tribes.

Once they reached Tennessee, the explorers traveled through what is now Washington County; tradition has it that they spent at least one night in the little cave near present-day Johnson City. They then turned south, eventually coming upon a village of Indians whom Gabriel Arthur identified as Tomahitans. The Tomahitans had already struck up an active trade with the Spanish in Florida, and they were more than happy to talk with the English about a similar agreement. Arthur, in his teens at the time, was left with the Tomahitans to learn their language while Needham returned to Colonel Wood with his report.

On the way back to Virginia, Needham and Indian John got into a violent argument, and before the Tomahitan guides could intervene, Indian John shot the Englishman dead. The Tomahitans were beside themselves in fear that the English would retaliate. But Indian John convinced them that they had to eliminate the other Englishman,

Gabriel Arthur, so no one could return to Colonel Wood and tell the story.

Upon returning to the Indian village, the Tomahitans discovered the chief was away. They hauled Arthur to the public square, tied him to a stake, and heaped armloads of combustibles at his feet. It looked as if the young explorer—not to mention any trade agreement with Colonel Wood—was about to go up in smoke.

Just then, the chief returned, a Spanish musket slung over his shoulder. He quickly discovered that Needham had been murdered and that Arthur was about to be broiled alive. A Waxhaw Indian—a visitor to the village—was about to torch the cane at Arthur's feet. The chief shouted for him to stop, but the Waxhaw was too worked up to listen to reason. The chief aimed his musket and shot the Waxhaw dead. Then he ran to Arthur, drew his knife, and cut the bonds. Arthur fled to the safety of the chief's lodge, while the chief dared anyone else in the village to molest the young Englishman.

After the furor died down, Arthur lived as one of the tribe, even accompanying the Tomahitans on raids. On a raid against the Shawnees in what is now West Virginia, he was wounded twice and captured by the enemy. It was about a year after Needham's death when Arthur was finally escorted back to Colonel Wood's trading post in Virginia.

The little cave near Johnson City continued to serve travelers as a resting and meeting place throughout the seventeenth and eighteenth centuries, though it was located far from any well-established Indian town. By the early eighteenth century, few Indians lived permanently in upper East Tennessee. The Cherokee, the dominant tribe in the area, banished smaller tribes shortly after the beginning of the century. The largest Cherokee towns were located to the southeast, in the Little Tennessee Valley. The tribe used upper East Tennessee mainly as a hunting ground.

The cave was a popular campsite because it was located near a famous Indian trail. Upper East Tennessee was honeycombed with trails, some no more than crudely cleared paths hacked through thick underbrush. But when Daniel Boone was laying out his Wilderness Road in 1769, he stumbled upon a long, wide, well-used trail that crossed the Holston River at Long Island. The trail extended from the general vicinity of Staunton, Virginia, to Echota, capital of the Cherokee nation, located between present-day Chattanooga and Chickamauga, Georgia. The trail, an Indian version of a superhighway, was called "the Great Path" by whites. Daniel Boone is said to have spent many nights in the little cave near Johnson City after he discovered the Great Path.

Upper East Tennessee was located at about the midpoint of the Great Path. When white settlers began entering the territory from North Carolina and the Shenandoah Valley, they gravitated toward this central area. Once they adopted the trail as their own highway through the wilderness, they often stopped overnight to rest in the little cave. Sometimes, Indians, white explorers, and settlers shared the cave at the same time.

Through times of peace and war, the cave sheltered travelers of all nations. One settler wrote about a night that the little cave housed a white family in front and a hunting party of a dozen Indians in the rear—all snoozing peacefully together. And at the mouth of the cave, a campfire crackled while a Cherokee brave and the white father sat and talked—or tried to communicate with each other in sign language—halfway through the night.

The cave extends back only thirty feet before it branches off into two main corridors, the left stretching about fifty feet and the right about thirty feet. The left-hand corridor ends at a sinkhole, perhaps fifteen feet deep. The right-hand corridor ends at a bare wall, with a small hole in the roof barely sufficient for a child to squeeze through. Inside, there is little to see as caves go—only a few scattered stalactites hang from the roof. But upper East Tennessee's Indians, explorers, and early settlers were not searching for caves of scenic splendor. Shelter was their priority, and the tiny cave offered plenty of that.

The cave is now part of the Tipton-Haynes Farm, a historical recreation area administered by the Johnson City Recreation Department. The restored white clapboard Tipton-Haynes House sits atop a hill just off the old Erwin Highway. Below the home are a springhouse and a pond complete with overfed ducks. Thirty yards to the east, across a well-manicured lawn and in plain sight of the main house, lies the cave. It is open to the public and is a favorite spot among children. Because of its size, there is no part of the cave from which the entrance is not plainly visible.

Those who visit on summer nights are sometimes treated to a kind of show that can't be seen in any theater. Some say the resident ghosts are those of Needham, Arthur, Indian John, and their Tomahitan guides from the expedition of 1673. Others claim to have seen the ghost of Daniel Boone. Once a welcome shelter for Indians and whites in centuries gone by, the little cave is now a unique meeting place of past and present.

Motifs: E 530.1. Ghostlike lights; E 402. Mysterious ghostlike noises heard; also E 402.1.1.7.* Ghost laughs; E 337. Ghost reenacts scene from own lifetime; E 422.4.5(b). Male revenant in old-fashioned garb; E 490. Meetings of the dead; E 425.2.4. Revenant as American Indian.

ECHOES
OF DEATH

In Unicoi County, near the upper end of Indian Creek, lush growths of pines and deciduous trees shade a sylvan bed of ferns and undergrowth. There, if one is still and listens carefully, screams can be heard echoing through the woods—the same kind of pained outcries that accompany sudden and horrible death. Of course, no one is really there—not a living soul. This is a world of phantoms, phantoms that keep alive a tragedy that befell the family of the county's earliest settler.

In late summer 1779, William Lewis and his family packed their belongings in North Carolina and set out for the promised land— the vast new western territory that lay across the mountains. Lewis chose a plot on the upper reaches of Indian Creek and cleared land to build a cabin for his wife and seven children. He had fine, strong sons. Together, they felled trees, notched logs, and soon built a serviceable cabin.

Not long after the family moved into its new home, the temperature dipped below the freezing mark—the first frost of autumn had come. The Lewises had packed enough provisions to last until spring planting. In the meantime, the woods were alive with squirrels, rabbits, and deer. William Lewis had brought plenty of firepower across the mountains, so his family had an abundance of fresh meat. Autumn was also a favorite hunting time for the Cherokee Indians. From their main camps to the south and southeast, they entered upper East Tennessee to hunt food for the winter. Hunting parties must have passed the Lewises' cabin from time to time and eyed the building and its occupants suspiciously, perhaps even nervously. The Indians knew from experience that one family of settlers begot more settlers. A steady stream of white families was beginning to inch westward, and they all seemed to feel they had rights to land the Indians had occupied for centuries. The Indians' relationship with whites was already becoming a string of broken promises, with the whites breaking any formal agreement reached by the two parties whenever it was to their advantage to do so.

The French and Indian War, in return, had taught settlers much about Indians. Indian attacks were often hit-and-run affairs, with the Indians doing as much damage as possible to the settlers before taking the shaken survivors—mostly women—as prisoners. Women and children were often adopted into the tribe. The most dangerous period for settlers was those few days after the first frost when unseasonably warm weather enveloped the forest. Known to the whites as "Indian summer," those days were the time the Indians were likeliest to attack.

By the middle of October, the Lewises were comfortably settled in their cabin for the winter. Their bins were full of corn, and dried meat hung in long brown strips from the rafters. A fireplace kept the cabin warm on chilly nights. Although the small cabin was crowded, the family knew that as they prospered they would be able to build a larger house, at which time the original cabin would be converted for use as a barn or a storage shed.

Early one morning, the forest was unnaturally quiet. No birds sang in the trees. Even the rushing water of Indian Creek had a different sound to it. And the weather was unnaturally warm. William Lewis, not suspecting anything was amiss, took advantage of the mild temperature to do a bit of fishing. Accompanied by his eldest son, he walked the short distance to the bank of Indian Creek and threw in his line.

Father and son had not been fishing long when a war whoop rent the air. Then screams rang out from the direction of the cabin. Lewis and his son threw down their lines, grabbed their muskets, and ran toward the house. By the time they arrived, the log cabin was in flames, and all around lay the crumpled bodies of the family members. Lewis drew his gun to the ready, but there was nothing to shoot at. The Indians had already melted into the forest.

His son glanced around, tears streaming down his face. "Lord God Almighty," he sobbed.

Lewis, too, was nearly beside himself with grief. His wife and children lay at his feet, their bodies bristling with arrows and gurgling blood. His four-year-old daughter's head was smashed in. His six-year-old son had been beaten to such an extent that his face was no longer recognizable. His wife had been stripped of her clothing and a crude knife had been plunged into her belly. The promised land had become one of horror and death.

Crushed, Lewis and his son began the sad task of burying the family. They could see the remains of one child inside the burning cabin, but they could not recover them until the fire had burnt itself out. Another child lay in the bushes behind the house.

"What manner of savage makes war on women and children?" Lewis asked himself angrily as he piled dirt onto the last grave, vowing swift justice for those who had murdered his family.

Then he discovered that his eldest daughter was missing. A thorough inspection of the cabin's ashes revealed no further trace of bones. Lewis searched the area surrounding the cabin, but no body was found. He suspected the daughter had been kidnapped by the Indians. After resting for a few hours, Lewis and his son took up their muskets and began to follow the Indian raiders.

Two nights later, the pair came upon a campsite where about a dozen Indians were gathered by a fire. In the flickering light, Lewis recognized his daughter—scared to death but apparently unhurt. His first inclination was to fire on the Indians in retaliation for the raid on the cabin. But there were only two white men and two muskets. All the other weapons had been destroyed in the fire. And the Indians could easily murder the girl if they were suddenly attacked.

Lewis decided to take a dangerous chance. Telling his son to remain hidden in case his plan failed, he sidestepped down the steep hill and calmly strolled into the camp, to the surprise of the unsuspecting Indians. At first, the Indians made threatening advances, muttering and poking at him with their weapons, but Lewis wisely kept his musket held high over his head. When his daughter saw him, she ran to him and threw her arms around him, nearly knocking him off-balance.

One of the Indians, probably the leader of the hunting party, asked Lewis what he wanted. After a few moments of trying to understand what was being said, Lewis laid down his musket and pointed to his daughter. "Her," he indicated.

The Indians understood immediately and shook their heads. They would not relinquish the girl. But then the leader of the party reached over and picked up Lewis's rifle. He had seen white men use the weapon before and was aware of its awesome power. The Indian indicated that he would be willing to trade the girl for the rifle. Although that would leave the three of them with only one weapon, Lewis readily agreed, also consenting to leave his full powder horn and a small supply of ammunition with the Indians. Without another word, Lewis and his daughter climbed the hill to where the surviving brother was crouched in hiding.

The Indians who had conducted the assault on the Lewis cabin were never seen or heard from again. When the three remaining family members crept back into the forest, it was to begin a new life in a new place. But the echoes of the tragic raid remain on upper Indian Creek in Unicoi County even today. Every once in a while, the scream of a child or a woman is heard echoing through the valley. Cries of anguish are sometimes heard in the forest, accompanied by an occasional bone-chilling war whoop. All the sounds are ghostly reminders of a horrible tragedy that took place long ago on a warm Indian-summer morning.

Motifs: E 402. Mysterious ghostlike noises heard; also E 337.1.1(n). Cries of family murdered by Indians are still heard.

LONG
ISLAND:
CURSED GROUND
OF THE CHEROKEE

The Indians who once used the Long Island of the Holston River for sacred ceremonies died long ago, but their voices can still be heard on moonlit nights—strange languages mixed with the antiquated English of eighteenth-century whites. On the now-polluted waters of the Holston in Kingsport, ghostly images of canoes and warriors are sometimes seen making shore on some long-forgotten peace mission. Ghostly campfires appear, surrounded by young braves and old warriors smoking the pipe of peace.

Two hundred years ago, a curse was placed upon the once-sacred ground of Long Island, thus making it unfit for habitation by white men. Even today, just being present on the island may encourage odd, sometimes violent behavior in people who in a different location would act quite normally.

A local tale is told about a man named Albert Ross, a sturdy and solid citizen of Kingsport who one night fell under the spell of the island.

During World War II, Ross's son, a marine, was on leave before being shipped to Europe. Young Ross and his girlfriend decided to spend a night on Long Island. A pillar of Christian piety, Albert Ross followed the pair, hoping to catch them in a romantic clinch.

All Albert Ross planned to do was scare the couple—everyone agrees on that fact. But seeing the couple in a compromising situation, he went berserk. He grabbed a stout tree limb and wielded it over his head as he ran toward the startled couple, who scrambled to their feet. The limb crashed heavily against young Ross's head, knocking him to the ground.

The girlfriend tried to back away, but Ross approached her next, screaming obscenities and threatening her with the club. Young Ross, his head bleeding, tried to stand but was unable to maintain his balance. He keeled over into unconsciousness.

Suddenly, Ross was upon the young lady—this creature of Satan who had seduced his son—and beat her viciously with the club. Bones cracked with each blow, and the girl, like her boyfriend, fell unconscious. As Ross stepped back to view his handiwork, reason returned. He let out a scream of horror that some folks say was heard for miles up and down the Holston River.

The next morning, the bodies of young Ross and his girlfriend were discovered on Long Island. Albert Ross was never found. Today, there is a legend on the island that Ross is still alive, still carrying his murderous club, and still seeking new victims. When he finds lovers on the island at night, he suddenly charges, wielding his terrible club of death.

How did the Long Island of the Holston come to inspire such behavior? What is its dark and checkered history, and what is the reason for the curse?

The history of the relationship between whites and the Cherokee is steeped in treachery. The first contact was friendly. When the Spanish explorer Hernando De Soto encountered the Cherokee in 1540, the Indians offered themselves as guides. Later, when De Soto turned on the Indians, murdering them by the score, the childlike trust turned to hate. Subsequent encounters between the Cherokee and whites became more and more unsavory. Bad relations festered over time and eventually exploded into open warfare.

Long Island is a good example of how the dealings between whites and Indians went sour. For hundreds of years, it had been against sacred Cherokee law for anyone to be killed or molested on the island—even whites. Solemn promises had been offered by one honorable person to another, one nation to another. Located on "the Great Path," Long Island was a central meeting ground for religious ceremonies and the creation of peace treaties.

But in the eighteenth century, during the eastern Indian wars, the Long Island of the Holston was considered strategic by first the British and then the Americans. In 1761, Fort Robinson was built by Colonel William Byrd on the north bank of the Holston River, opposite the east end of Long Island. The fort garrisoned colonial troops to protect settlers against Indian attacks. It was large and well-provisioned for its time, and it intimidated the Indians. Shortly after Fort Robinson was completed, about four hundred Cherokee led by Atakullakulla—or "Little Carpenter," as the whites called him—arrived to talk peace with the white soldiers.

That peace did not last long. The winter of 1768–69 saw an influx of settlers who claimed land as far south as Boones Creek. Once again, the Cherokee became edgy; the more settlers there were on their hunting ground, the less game there was for the Cherokee to hunt. Warfare broke out once more, and Long Island was again the focus of activity.

On August 1, 1776, the Virginia Council of Defense, by the authority of Governor Patrick Henry, ordered Colonel William Christian and two battalions of soldiers to move against the Cherokee to the south. Christian's troops joined North Carolina troops under Major Winston at Long Island. In the meantime, the Cherokee chiefs, confident of the worthiness of their warriors, bragged that the whites would never cross the French Broad River.

By October, Christian had mobilized two thousand men and accumulated more than enough firepower to fight any force the Indians could assemble. Among the colonial forces, there was even a company of cavalry under the command of Major John Sevier, later to become a hero at the battle of Kings Mountain. The war with the Indians had swung in favor of the whites before it even began.

Early in October, the push south began. Christian and his forces swept over the countryside with sheer numbers and overwhelming firepower. The Indians fled in terror, offering little or no resistance.

By November, the Cherokee were ready to sue for peace. The whites accepted, but British soldiers remained in Indian country for over six months as a peacekeeping force.

On July 2, 1777, Cherokee chiefs and white soldiers sat down at the Long Island of the Holston to discuss a lasting peace. After three weeks of talks and a seemingly endless procession of Indian ceremonies, the treaty was finally signed on July 20. It assigned certain areas of western North Carolina to be exclusively Indian. Other territories were to be the exclusive property of whites. One territory the Indians lost was Long Island itself.

The Cherokee were saddened at being forced to give up their sacred ground. Relinquishing an important part of their heritage to the whites was a devastating loss. Still, it was better than suffering certain death at the hands of an invader better organized and possessing superior firepower.

Shortly after the treaty was signed, the Cherokee left their sacred island for the last time, but not until a disgruntled medicine man cursed the ground. Summoning evil spirits of the dead with weird chants and incantations, he decreed that no white man would ever live again on the island in peace.

Once again, it did not take the whites long to break the treaty signed on Long Island. There were just too many settlers moving into the area to allow the Indians exclusive territory. When whites reinvaded land they had promised the Cherokee, the Indians fought back. Sporadic fighting between Indians and settlers continued until 1796, but the Indians' cause was star-crossed. The number of incoming settlers was just too overwhelming.

Today, little remains of the island's wilderness as it once was. The Long Island of the Holston River is now a national historic landmark. On one end of the island, there is a park. On the other, Tennessee Eastman has built a waste-disposal plant.

Law-enforcement officials will tell you that some of the worst local problems occur on the island. Crimes seem to occur more frequently there than in other areas of Kingsport. Since the Indians gave up Long Island, whites have robbed, fought, and murdered each other there, often without knowing why—Albert Ross's murderous spree is only one example. It is as if the lunacy of the full moon forever hangs over the island, driving ordinary people to do extraordinary things.

Motifs: E 402. Mysterious ghostlike noises heard; E 425.2.4. Revenant as American Indian; E 530.1. Ghostlike lights; E 490. Meetings of the dead.

A
PLACE OF TERROR:
ROTHERWOOD
MANSION

Rotherwood Mansion, a magnificent home overlooking the Holston River, boasts both one of the most gentle and one of the most terrifying ghosts in upper East Tennessee. One is the apparition of a beautiful young woman who never recovered from the tragedy of a lost love. The other is the ghost of an unbelievably cruel man who died a horrible death and whose remains refused to be buried.

Rotherwood was built in 1818 by Frederick A. Ross, a gifted man of unquenchable energy. Ross laid out the town of Rossville—which eventually became Kingsport—and a town called Christianville. He also built the first bridge over the North Fork of the Holston River. A gentleman farmer, Ross made Rotherwood a successful plantation. In addition to his other accomplishments, he was ordained a minister in 1825. Ross and Rotherwood seemed destined for success, but tragedy gnawed at the master of Rotherwood Mansion like a hungry wolf.

His daughter, Rowena, was a Southern belle whose beauty and grace were legendary. She was educated in the finest Northern schools and was an accomplished musician and a charming hostess. Everyone liked and admired her. She seemed blessed by the gods.

Rowena had been out of school only two years when she became engaged to a young man from a neighboring community. The day before the wedding, guests arrived in droves, staying at Rotherwood and other homes in the area. The occasion was a festive time for everyone. Kingsport's princess was to marry her Prince Charming in the social event of the season. All the local gentry wanted to be on hand.

The afternoon before the wedding, Rowena's young fiancé and several friends embarked on a fishing trip in a small boat on the Holston River. Almost directly in front of the house, and in plain sight of Rowena, the flimsy vessel capsized. Rowena hurried down the hill toward the fishermen floundering in the water, but she was too late. All were saved except her fiancé. An hour later, his sodden body was pulled from the murky water.

The tragedy greatly affected Rowena. She became semireclusive. Two years later, she pulled herself together enough to marry a wealthy man from Knoxville. Soon after the marriage, he died of yellow fever. Ten years later, Rowena once again reached for happiness, this time marrying Edward Temple of Huntsville, Alabama. This last marriage yielded one child, a daughter Rowena named after her mother, and it appeared that stability had finally come into her life. But when her daughter was six or seven years old, Rowena committed suicide. It was not long after that when "the Lady in White" began to be seen at Rotherwood.

Rowena Ross is the most frequently sighted ghost at Rotherwood. For over 125 years, she has been spotted, usually dressed in white, wandering the banks of the Holston River, apparently searching for her drowned lover. She has been seen by hundreds of people, among them the famous George Eastman and financier John B. Dennis.

"One of the people I talked to who saw Rowena was in front of the mansion house picking strawberries," said Dr. Nancy Acuff, a professor at East Tennessee State University and an expert on local ghost lore. "He was a small child at the time and is now a physician in Kingsport. He was kneeling on the ground when the Lady in White walked by him. To him, it was a terrifying moment. He knew it was not real, but he saw her coming and then stand beside him. Ever since, he has lived in dread of ever seeing her again."

Rowena's gentle ghost was already well-established when tragedy once again gnawed at Frederick Ross. He fell into dire financial straits in November 1847 and found it necessary to sell his mansion and nineteen hundred acres of land to the notorious Joshua Phipps. It is the ghost of Joshua Phipps—Rotherwood's second ghost—that is responsible for giving the estate its infamous ghostly reputation.

Phipps, a successful farmer who owned about forty slaves, was a diehard antiabolitionist. He was also known to have a cruel streak two miles wide. Neighbors remembered the harsh way he treated his slaves, their screams of pain echoing throughout the countryside whenever he beat them.

Rotherwood prospered under Phipps until the first year of the Civil War. Tennessee experienced an especially hot summer that year. Humidity hung like a pall over the countryside. Joshua Phipps fell gravely ill and was not expected to live. He lay on his bed in the carriage house of his estate, his shallow breathing contrasting horribly with the singing of birds outside the open windows. At the head of his bed sat a small black boy whose job it was to fan his master. Suddenly, according to legend, a swarm of flies entered through the unscreened windows and landed on the dying man's face. More and more insects arrived every second, crawling into the open mouth and nostrils of Joshua Phipps. Soon, Phipps had difficulty breathing. The young slave stopped his fanning and watched the fascinating spectacle. The old man choked and gasped for air. In a few minutes, Joshua Phipps was dead—strangled by hundreds of flies—while the slave laughed at the sight of his dreaded master giving up the ghost in such an unceremonious manner.

The death of Joshua Phipps may have ended the terror suffered by his slaves, but it also marked the beginning of a different kind of terror at Rotherwood Mansion. On July 10, hundreds of mourners and curiosity seekers assembled at Rotherwood for the funeral services and burial. The body was brought out of the mansion to a waiting caisson in the circular driveway. Once the casket was loaded, the caisson would haul the body up a hill to the cemetery.

Nancy Acuff, whose grandfather attended the funeral, told the rest of the story. "Just as the procession was preparing to move, they noticed that the sky had become noticeably darker, and they were hoping that the minister would be short of speech at the grave site," she said. "The caisson driver snapped the reins, the horses pulled with all of their might, but they simply could not move the caisson. They stood absolutely still. They were frozen.

"Then one of the slave boys said that he would bring up a better team of horses. They uncoupled the old team and backed in the new. The caisson driver tipped his hat in respect to the widow. He snapped the reins again and the horses started off. They pulled and jerked and pulled and jerked, but still could not move the caisson more than just a few feet. The wheels simply would not turn.

"By this time, everyone was mumbling among themselves and wondering what was going on. Everyone was embarrassed, and no one knew quite what to do. One of the men in the crowd cried out that he had brought his Percherons with him, and he volunteered these huge workhorses to pull the caisson. So he rushed over, brought his horses, and hitched them up to the caisson.

"The driver snapped the reins for the third time, and these Percherons pulled the caisson up the side of the hill, up toward the cemetery. They got about halfway up the hill and these huge horses were actually pulling the soil out of the ground as they tried to move the casket up to the graveyard.

"The sky was getting blacker and darker and everyone was getting anxious at the thought of the oncoming storm. Suddenly, a bolt of lightning shot through the sky, and there was a rumble of thunder, and a whoosh of cold wind went out over the entire assembly. A rustling sound was heard over the casket. The canopy covering the coffin began to move. An enormous black dog jumped out from underneath the canopy and went racing off over the hillside. Everyone stood there in absolute total silence.

"The story goes that this 'Hound of Hell' can be heard many nights—especially on stormy nights—wandering among the shrubs and dashing through the bushes at Rotherwood, crying out mournfully."

After Joshua Phipps was buried, the crowd of mourners and curiosity seekers dispersed to their homes. As word of the strange happenings at the funeral spread around the area, it was naturally assumed by residents that the ghost of Joshua Phipps would haunt Rotherwood Mansion. They were right.

Nancy Acuff's father used to tell her of visits he made to Rotherwood with her grandfather. "They would ride up here from Rogersville to visit," she said. "He said that you couldn't sleep in Rotherwood Mansion at night. He said that old Joshua roamed the halls, and if you would lie down, he would be at the foot of the bed at midnight yanking the covers off and laughing that horrible screaming laugh of his. For months and months following Phipps's death, the house was just a place of terror."

Little is written of Joshua Phipps in the histories of Sullivan County and Kingsport, although much can be found concerning Frederick Ross. This seems an odd turn, since Phipps was an important local landowner and must have been an influential person. It has proven difficult to determine the exact reason behind this. Perhaps Sullivan County is ashamed of its former resident. Perhaps the feeling is that the less said about Joshua Phipps, the better.

Motifs: E 281. Ghosts haunt house; E 334.2.3. Ghost of tragic lover haunts scene of tragedy; E 334.2.3(b). Ghost of a young woman who died a tragic lover; E 334.2.3(ce). Ghost of woman who had lost lover tragically during her lifetime; E 422.4.4(a). Female revenant in white clothing; F 956. Premature darkness; D 2072. Magical paralysis; D 1654.9. Corpse in coffin refuses to be moved in wagon; G 303.3.3.3.1.1. The devil in the form of a dog; E 421.3.6. Ghosts as dogs with glowing tongues and eyes; E 423(a). Spirit animal, revenant in animal form; E 402. Mysterious ghostlike sounds heard; E 279.3. Ghost pulls bedclothing from sleeper.

THE
HAINTED
RIVER

"This river really is hainted," the old man said as he stood by the muddy, trash-strewn bank of the Nolichucky River. Then he added sadly, "There was a time when the river didn't look so much like a slop bucket. She was clean and free. You could fish anywhere along the banks here and you didn't have to throw rusty beer cans out of your way to get to the water. Damned shame what's happened to her. Bunch of kids did this. One day, one of them haints is gonna rise up on one of those litterbugs and scare the hell out of him."

The old man was right about the condition of the river. The sparkling waters of the Nolichucky were once a godsend to early settlers in Washington and Greene counties, but some areas along the river are now in danger of looking more like the setting for one of the "toxic monster" stories that have gained so much popularity in comic books and movies.

He was also right about the dark, haunted side of the river. The Nolichucky is a dangerous swimming hole filled with hidden rocks and crevices, swirling eddies, and treacherous undertows. There are dozens of stories about the ghosts of unfortunate swimmers who drowned in the river. In fact, all kinds of apparitions are witnessed along the banks, from visions of young girls, to the ghost of Daniel Boone, to banshees, to the sound of phantom hoofbeats.

For example, there is the story of Flora Turner, a red-haired girl who became a victim of the Nolichucky's dangerous currents during the Great Depression. Flora's ghost has sometimes been seen running nude along the banks of the river.

Flora had fallen in love with a young man from the Chucky community. A wedding was planned, and the young man, a farmer, was in the process of building a cottage for his future bride on a corner of his father's farm. One night, the pair decided to go skinny-dipping in the Nolichucky. Tragically, Flora drowned, and her body was never recovered.

Two nights after her death, the fiancé went to the river to brood. The night was dark and moonless, but the water still stood out from the banks on either side. There was an odd light shining on everything—it had no particular source, but was heavy and diffused, like sunlight bleeding through a parasol.

Suddenly, the young man felt a cold chill, an oppressive feeling, a strong sensation that someone was behind him. He wheeled around but saw nothing. He turned again to the river and felt the chill once more. Turning away again, he saw what appeared to be Flora, quietly standing in a little clump of scrubby trees and watching him. He was flabbergasted. He knew she was dead and that what he was seeing could not possibly be. When he called her name and stepped toward her, she faded from view. It was then he knew that he had seen Flora's ghost. In the intervening years, Flora has been seen along the banks of the Nolichucky at night by a variety of people.

Another tale concerns the occasional sighting of a hunter garbed in buckskin and armed with an ancient fowling piece who roams the woods near the river. He is most often seen in the area near where the Chucky Trading Post now stands. Locals believe he is the spirit of either Daniel Boone—the preferred choice—or noted patriot and soldier John Sevier, who owned land nearby. It is difficult to find anyone today who has actually seen the hunter, but a number of local people learned the story from their fathers and grandfathers, who claimed to have seen the apparition.

Another tradition claims that the Nolichucky is the home of a bona fide Irish banshee. In Celtic legend, a banshee is a spirit whose wail warns a family of an approaching death. Many early settlers along the Nolichucky were Ulster Scots (people of Scotch-Irish ancestry) who probably were well-acquainted with the Old World legend of the banshee. Sometimes at night, an eerie cry was heard near the river.

One old man who lives in a shack near the bank had a personal experience with the banshee; he heard it only once, but once was enough for him. The man was a trapper. In the early 1930s, he was young and happily married to one of the local girls. She was pregnant with their first child, and the couple was eagerly awaiting their blessed event.

One night, the man was checking his traps along the river when he heard a wail. His first impression was that it was a wildcat. As he tracked the sound, hoping to obtain a valuable new pelt, the wail remained constant—neither growing louder nor fading away. After two hours of fruitless searching for its source, the trapper finally gave up.

Returning to the cabin, he found to his horror that his wife was giving birth to their child—by herself. There was no telephone, and the nearest neighbor was about a half-mile away. The husband tried to help with the birth, but the baby was emerging breech first. The child was stillborn, and the young woman died a few minutes later.

As the old man told his story, tears formed in the corners of his eyes. "I know now that what I heard in them woods was a banshee," he said. "My grandfather had told me about the banshee and its cry. And it was tryin' to tell me to get back home to my wife. But instead, I spent two hours chasin' what I thought was a wildcat. If I had only listened to what the thing was a-tryin' to tell me."

Perhaps the most unsettling tale about the Nolichucky concerns a spooky stretch of river near Bumpass Cove and the former town of Poleville, a mining area since the late eighteenth century. Occasionally, witnesses hear the pounding of hooves along the bank, but no horse or rider appears. Furthermore, there is no clear path along the river on which a person might ride. The whole bank is covered with dense, tangled undergrowth and is quite impassable. Yet the sound is often heard on moonlit nights. At first, it is far off in the distance, then it steadily rises as it approaches, then it passes by the listener and recedes in the distance. Only a glimpse of a black, shadowy form can be seen.

Over the years, there has been much speculation over the source of the sound. Some think it is the ghost of an Indian riding to warn his brethren of approaching white soldiers. Others have blacker thoughts about the origin of the sound. For them, the most blood-thirsty warrior would be no match for the evil spirit that regularly runs the bank of the Nolichucky.

The story of the haunting of Bumpass Cove began to surface in the 1920s. Residents along the river would hear the sound of hoof-beats coming toward them in the middle of the night, peer out of their windows, and see a black shadow moving along the bank at terrific speed. Then, as quickly as the apparition appeared, it would be gone. For a long time, residents tried to discover the source of the disturbance. Finally, they gave up and assumed that what they were seeing and hearing was a ghost. Since the haunt confined itself to the riverbank, most residents felt they had nothing to fear. But as in every community infested with a ghost, there were those who were bound and determined to solve the mystery.

One Saturday night, a group of men, well into their cups, decided to go down to the river and wait for the phantom horseman to appear. Certain they were dealing with no ghost, the men arrived armed with ropes they intended to use to trip the horse and spill its rider. One man even had a gun and was talking of shooting the rider out of the saddle. As the evening wore on, the men got drunker. It was a beautiful night. Moonbeams reflected like gems on the water. Finally, at about ten o'clock, hoofbeats were heard in the distance.

Quickly, the men began stretching the rope along the ground, tying one end to a scrub tree at the water's edge and extending the rope back about thirty feet from the river. They pulled it taut, hoping that the horse's hocks would become entangled and that both horse and rider would fall into a tangled heap.

They waited. The sound of hoofbeats came nearer, but the horse was not yet in sight. Noting the thick growth of bushes along the water's edge, the men wondered how a horse could run with such obstacles blocking its path.

In an instant, the hoofbeats were upon them—then passed by. The rope suddenly stretched like something had hit it at great speed. All the men holding it were upended and sprawled on the ground, enmeshed in prickly briers. The hoofbeats receded in the distance as the men picked themselves up, cursing and pulling thistles from their overalls.

One of the men, perhaps the most sober of the group, ran down to the water's edge. Briers and undergrowth were spread on the ground like a tangled carpet. Nothing could have possibly passed unimpeded. But the bushes were not even broken.

Suddenly, someone gave a yell and pointed to the ground. There in the moonlight, beneath one particularly scrubby specimen of undergrowth, was a hoofprint—then another and another. The men gathered around, gawking at the discovery. Something really had gone by, avoided their trap, and left a visible record of its passing. Their first impulse was to congratulate themselves for solving the mystery—ghosts don't leave hoofprints, so their "ghost" was obviously no ghost at all.

Then someone noticed something odd about the prints. They were much smaller than that of a horse, and not rounded like a horse's. The prints were about the size of a goat's, and they were cloven!

When the men realized what they were looking at, they fled back to their homes as fast as their legs could carry them. This was no ghost who ran the banks of the Nolichucky River—it was the devil himself!

Phantom hoofbeats are still heard along the Nolichucky, but after that night, no one has ever dared to find out who or what is making the racket. From that night onward, the little stretch of the Nolichucky River at Bumpass Cove has been known as "Devil's Run."

Motifs: E 334(d). Ghost runs up and down bank (cf. E 334. Non-malevolent ghost haunts scene of former misfortunes, crime, or tragedy); E 422.4.5(b). Male revenant in old-fashioned garb; D 1812.5. Future learned through omens; D 1827.1.3. Noise warns of approaching death; E 421.1. Invisible ghost; E 402.1.2. Footsteps of invisible ghost heard; E 402.2.3. Hoofbeats of ghost horse; E 599.5. Ghost travels swiftly; E 265. Meeting ghost causes misfortune; E 544. Ghost leaves evidence of his appearance; G 303.4.5.4. Devil has cloven goat hoof.

THE
GHOSTLY
JACKSONS OF
JONESBOROUGH

Jonesborough is the oldest town in Tennessee, with the possible exception of the Watauga settlement in Carter County and Trade in Johnson County. It must also contain more ghosts per capita than any other city or town in upper East Tennessee. Ghost stories are so plentiful that recording them all would take a volume twice this size.

There is more to the plethora of spooks than just the fact that Jonesborough is Tennessee's oldest town. The town is so firmly planted on history's stage and some of its inhabitants were so eccentric that there were bound to be legends and wild tales.

Much of the early history of Tennessee occurred in and around Jonesborough. The stage was set in 1779, when the North Carolina General Assembly passed legislation leading to the establishment of the first permanent settlement in the newly formed Washington District of western North Carolina. Jonesborough—named in honor of Willie (pronounced Wiley) Jones, a patriot and statesman from Halifax, North Carolina—became the first permanent town on the western slope of the Appalachian Mountains. In 1780, the town was surveyed and laid out by John Gilliland, who was paid $1,115 for the job. Settlers moved in, and Jonesborough flourished.

Politically, Jonesborough was an important settlement in its first years, often proving itself a thorn in the side of the North Carolina government. The state government insisted that residents of the new district be levied a full share of taxes, but it neglected to defend settlers against Indian attacks. The state also refused to honor any treaties or business transactions settlers made directly with the Indians. Frustrated with an unresponsive government, some settlers decided that it was time to secede from North Carolina and apply to the United States Congress for statehood.

On August 23, 1784, delegates from Washington, Sullivan, and Greene counties met in Jonesborough to plan a new state, to be called the "State of Franklin." The move ensured that federal troops would be sent to assist in the Indian wars. Six months later, a second convention was held in Jonesborough to adopt a constitution. The next year, a meeting in Greeneville chose John Sevier as governor and Jonesborough as the state capital.

Sevier was a local celebrity—a leader of the Overmountain Men during the Revolutionary War, a hero of the battle of Kings Mountain, and an early settler along the banks of the Nolichucky River. But he had bitter opponents. Colonel John Tipton, a man who remained loyal to the government of North Carolina, was a sworn enemy of Sevier and the effort to organize a new state. One day, while Sevier was out of town fighting Indians, Tipton and his supporters chased the State of Franklin's magistrates out of the courthouse in Jonesborough and installed a government loyal to Tipton's philosophy. A bench warrant was then issued for John Sevier on a charge of treason. The new government ultimately fell apart, and by 1788 the State of Franklin was only a memory. Ironically, when Tennessee became a bona fide state in 1798, the "traitor" Sevier became its first governor.

Jonesborough remained a center of activity through the years that followed. Some of the most notable activity centered around two famous men named Jackson who lived and worked in Jonesborough during the nineteenth century. Each has a number of ghostly tales associated with his name. One Jackson was a Civil War general and the other a future president of the United States.

Andrew Jackson, the town's foremost spook, arrived in Jonesborough from Morganton, North Carolina, in the spring of 1788 to set up a law practice. He stayed only six months before leaving to look for greener pastures in Nashville. It was a full decade before he returned, this time to sit on the bench of the superior court of the state of Tennessee. It was from his years as judge that the Jonesborough legends surrounding Jackson arose.

The two-fisted justice practiced by Jackson, a backwoodsman turned lawyer, gave birth to a host of anecdotes. Noted for his quick and violent temper, Jackson conducted his business on the same primitive level as many of the offenders who approached his bench. His style was a matter of necessity, because in those days Jonesborough was a rough-and-ready town, much like Dodge City, Kansas, and Tombstone, Arizona, would later become.

While presiding over one case in Jonesborough in 1802, Jackson performed as judge, arresting officer, and one-man posse. The accused, Russell Bean, was the son of Captain William Bean, the first permanent settler in Tennessee. Russell Bean was also the first white child born in the state. But those distinctions did not give him a noble character. Bean committed the dastardly act of cutting off the ears of a child he was accused of—but denied—fathering. The child later died from its injuries.

Jackson issued a warrant for Bean's arrest, but Bean refused to be arrested. Washington County Sheriff John Couch failed to pursue the matter, informing Jackson of Bean's refusal of the county's hospitality. Jackson ordered Couch to form a posse to capture Bean, but no one in town would volunteer, since Bean was extremely popular in Washington County. The enraged Jackson then ordered Sheriff Couch to order some men to volunteer, whereupon Couch conscripted Jackson himself. Overcome with fury, Jackson declared that, "by the Eternal," he would confiscate the nearest pistol and capture Bean himself.

A few hours later, Jackson confronted Bean, and the latter, noting the grim determination in the judge's eye, surrendered without a struggle. He was promptly dragged into court and convicted, though he escaped with a light sentence, considering he was charged with the murder of a child. Bean was branded on the left thumb and jailed for eleven months.

Jackson was more than equal to living and working in Jonesborough. Drunkenness was rampant. Street fights broke out daily. Men stabbed, shot, or killed each other over nothing more earthshaking than a deal of the cards. Jackson dispensed justice frontierstyle, in spite of a vocal and sometimes abusive audience. When the ruckus in the courtroom became too much, he drew his pistol and placed it on the bench, daring anyone to disturb the dignity of his court. On one occasion, during the trial of a man accused of stealing a horse, there was so much disorder in the court that Jackson was forced to fire his pistol at the ceiling, instead of rapping his gavel, to restore order.

It is difficult to tell when the stories of Jackson's ghost began, but they have been around for many years. One story concerns the Christopher Taylor House, where Jackson lived while he practiced law in town. The house was later moved from its original location, a mile outside the city limits, and is now the centerpiece of Jonesborough's municipal park. The ghost of Andy Jackson is said to haunt the two-story log building. Witnesses have sworn that Jackson's shade can be seen walking from the rear to the front of the house. The ghost pauses at the door for a moment—as if contemplating whether to enter—and eventually walks inside.

Some claim that Jackson's shade is best seen on foggy nights. One man, a longtime resident of the town, said that he was out walking late one evening when he saw a figure dressed in old-fashioned garb emerge from behind the Christopher Taylor House and move to the front door. Under one of the ghost's arms was a stack of papers, and under the other a pair of saddlebags. Almost instinctively, the eyewitness knew he was seeing the ghost of Andy Jackson, and when the spirit turned in his direction before entering the house, its face proved the point.

On other occasions, Jackson has been seen striding along Main Street in front of a former hotel, rushing in the general direction of the old courthouse. These sightings are interesting for two reasons.

First, all such sightings have occurred in broad daylight. Second, in every such instance, Jackson's ghost has been seen by people walking on the opposite side of the street, but never by those on the same side of the street—not even by people passing within inches of the apparition.

In Jonesborough, there is an assumption that every unexplained event can be blamed on the shade of Andrew Jackson. There is a story, for example, that Jackson haunts the home of Burgin Dossett, retired president of East Tennessee State University. Dossett's home is known as "Febuary Hill." The brick building was constructed in 1832 for Congressman John Blair and was later owned by Alexander D. Febuary, a tailor. The home remained in the Febuary family for generations until it was sold to Dossett.

When Dossett and his wife, Nell, moved into the house, the electricity had not yet been turned on, and they had to use candles for light. Before retiring for bed one evening, the Dossetts inadvertently left a candle burning dangerously close to draperies in the living room. In the morning, Dossett discovered that the candle, instead of burning down and setting fire to the draperies, had been snuffed out—obviously so. There was no one else in the house that night. Dossett eventually came to believe that it was Andrew Jackson's ghost who saved his home. Jackson supposedly haunts the garden at Febuary Hill as well.

General Alfred "Mudwall" Jackson, the second of Jonesborough's famous Jacksons, arrived on the scene a bit later than Andy. His ghost has not actually been seen in Jonesborough, but his activities during the Civil War are said to be partly responsible for the supernatural infestation of the town's most infamous haunted house.

Alfred Jackson's father, Samuel Jackson, arrived in Jonesborough in 1801, but finding the town at odds with his genteel nature, he almost immediately removed himself to land he owned near Nashville. Samuel Jackson was a good friend of Andrew Jackson, and he shared the latter's penchant for horse racing. In 1811, Andy won ten thousand acres of Samuel's best land in a horse race. Samuel, a poor loser, tried to kill "Old Hickory," but the feisty general ran him through with a cane spear. Samuel recovered but was so upset over the incident that he did not speak to Andy for several years. Eventually, all was forgiven, and the two became friends again.

Young Alfred Jackson attended Washington and Greeneville colleges before entering business with his father. In 1842, he took up permanent residence in Jonesborough, where he opened a large store four years later. Alfred was a first-class promoter and financier. He was one of those who encouraged the building of the East Tennessee and Virginia Railway.

In 1861, Alfred Jackson joined the Confederate army and became a quartermaster and paymaster. By 1862, Washington County was under Confederate control. Jackson was commissioned a major and assigned to the staff of General Felix Zollicoffer. A short time later, he obtained a field command. Jackson was not a military man, but rather a political general—a highly respected businessman who had done many favors for those in power. He was also a close friend and a relative, by marriage, of Jefferson Davis. Once he was made a general, Jackson was given the nickname "Mudwall" so he would not be confused with the more famous General Stonewall Jackson of Virginia.

Mudwall Jackson offered to command the newly organized Sixtieth Tennessee Infantry. In the meantime, he was given command of all of upper East Tennessee and headquartered in Bristol. When Union General Ambrose Burnside marched into Knoxville early in 1863, he sent troops northward to test the strength of the Confederate forces in Washington and Sullivan counties. Jackson sent a force southward that engaged Federal forces at the Embree House in Telford. After a short battle, the Union troops retreated six miles south to Limestone Depot. The Confederates followed, and after two and a half hours of heavy artillery shelling, Union forces surrendered. Those captured were sent to Richmond, Virginia, as prisoners of war.

During battles in and around Jonesborough, Jackson's home—a large, rambling brick house overlooking the town—was used as a hospital. The carnage of Civil War battles is notorious. The low-velocity minie balls used by both sides tore ragged holes in flesh, infecting their victims with a host of germs. Wounds festered, and soldiers not killed outright on the battlefield were often felled by complications. When gangrene set in, the practice was to remove the limb rather than try to save it. Plenty of whiskey was available, but it was poured into the man, not into the wound as an antiseptic. It is not known exactly how many soldiers died horribly in the Jackson House, but the number was high.

Parapsychologists—those who conduct scientific studies of the supernatural—are quick to point out why the Jackson House should be inhabited by ghosts. Indeed, most old houses used as military hospitals are haunted. Wherever severe trauma and pain have occurred, ghosts are likely to be most active.

In 1875, Nathan Morrell and his wife were living in the Jackson House. Morrell, a Jonesborough businessman, had rented the place from Jackson. Almost from the beginning, the couple was plagued by poltergeists. According to the weekly *Jonesborough Herald and Tribune*, the first episode of ghostly activity began when Nathan heard footsteps on the floor above him. The sound was like that of a man walking with a cane. As he and his wife huddled in the parlor, they heard the footsteps travel from one side of the room above to the other. Next, they descended the stairs, then, after a moment, returned to the upper floor. Each time, Morrell investigated the sound, but he found nothing.

That was only the beginning. One night, Mrs. Morrell was alone reading in her room on the second floor when the footsteps began. By that time, the Morrells had become accustomed to the sound, so after listening for a few moments, she returned to her reading. She knew if she went into the hall to investigate, she would find nothing.

The footsteps stopped in front of her closed bedroom door. Mrs. Morrell glanced up from her book and was horrified to see the doorknob begin to turn. "Nathan, is that you?" she called out.

There was no answer.

"Nathan! Answer me!" she cried.

The knob stopped turning. Suddenly, a violent banging shook the door and reverberated through the house. Mrs. Morrell screamed. Whatever haunted the house was trying to get into her bedroom.

She screamed again, even louder than before, and the banging stopped.

A heart-pounding moment passed. Then the doorknob began turning again. Mrs. Morrell watched in silent terror. She jumped like a scalded cat when the door burst open and Nathan ran to her bedside. When she told him the story, he volunteered to look for the intruder. He said, however, that he had not heard the footsteps or the pounding—just his wife's screaming. That was why he had come.

Mrs. Morrell grabbed her husband's arm. "No," she said, shaking with fright. "Don't go. Don't leave me."

Morrell put his arms around his wife to comfort her. It was then that both husband and wife thought they heard a wailing that sounded like a despondent woman crying in grief.

Another story about the haunting of the Jackson House concerns one of the Morrells' children. By the time Nathan and his wife began experiencing the ghosts, their children were grown and living on their own. One son, Elbert, lived on a nearby farm and often visited his mother and father. He had heard them talk about the ghostly noises in the house but had never witnessed anything himself.

Elbert again visited his parents, but this time he heard a mysterious scratching sound that seemed to be coming from somewhere inside the walls. An inspection revealed nothing. "Mice," Elbert said confidently, dismissing the incident. His parents were not so sure.

A few minutes later, Elbert and his parents were deep in conversation. Then, without warning, the chair Elbert was sitting in rose six inches into the air, and a loud report, as though the chair had been struck by a board, reverberated through the house. The chair crashed back to the floor, bearing a stunned and flabbergasted Elbert. Nothing was said for a moment. Everyone was too shocked. Then the elder Morrell turned toward his wife, an amused expression on his face. "Mice," he said, nodding his head.

The ghosts in the Jackson House at that time did not include that of Mudwall himself, who lived well into the 1880s. Once he died, old-timers around Jonesborough began saying that Mudwall's ghost had joined those of the tortured soldiers already in residence.

Local tradition says the house became so infamous that the owners were unable to find tenants to live in it. If the story printed in the *Herald and Tribune* is true—and there is no reason to believe Nathan Morrell would lie just to open himself up to the ridicule of the community—then the Jackson House was truly a place infested by spirits. The demolition of the house shortly after the turn of the century may have ended the noisy activities within, but some spirits linger. At night, a crying woman can still be heard on the hillside—an unsettling reminder of Jonesborough's most haunted house.

Motifs: E 338. Non-malevolent ghost haunts building; E 422.4.5(b). Male revenant in old-fashioned garb; 339.1.* Non-malevolent ghost haunts spot of former activity or spot for which he has some affection; E 337. Ghost reenacts scene from own lifetime; E 363.2. Ghost returns to protect the living; F 473.2.3. Spirit puts out lights; E 363.1. Ghost aids living in emergency; E 402.1.2. Footsteps of invisible ghost heard; E 402. Mysterious ghostlike noises heard; E 338.1(aa). Ghost knocks on door; E 338.1(c). Ghost opens doors and windows repeatedly; E 402.1.1.2. Ghost moans; E 402.1.5(a). Ghost knocks on furniture; E 281.0.3. Ghost haunts house, damaging property or annoying inhabitants.

THE
GHOST WHO
CRIED FOR HELP

Boys the world over love to take dares—that's an undeniable fact. A night spent in a haunted house, or any other location supposedly infested by a ghost, is the kind of dare that no self-respecting young man can resist, especially when pressed by his peers. A favorite spot for this kind of sport in upper East Tennessee is a copse of a half-dozen elm and oak trees near Piney Flats, located about halfway between Johnson City and Bristol. There, the horrible apparition of a wounded Union soldier once pleaded piteously for help, his red eyes glowing with the fires of hell.

The legend of the ghost who cried for help had its beginnings in September 1863. Union troops under the command of General Ambrose Burnside set upon a force of Confederates assembled in Washington County. After a skirmish, Union troops retired, thinking they had soundly whipped the Confederates. A portion of the Union force was left to guard an important bridge across Little Limestone Creek, while the remaining soldiers returned to Greeneville by train.

The Confederates were not beaten quite so easily. Their ranks swelled by reinforcements from Jonesborough, they attacked the Yankees at the bridge. For a time, a Confederate victory seemed imminent. But Union troops increased their fire, aided by twelve-pound Napoleon smooth-bore cannons, and the Southerners were forced to retreat to the Greene County line.

Two weeks later, Confederate forces again engaged Union troops in and around Jonesborough, the county seat of Washington County. A running battle ensued that extended from Jonesborough northward through Johnson's Depot (later Johnson City) and on toward Bluff City. Scattered groups of men on both sides stalked each other, blazing away from behind trees, rock outcroppings, and riverbanks. Confederate sharpshooters, most of whom had gained their skills by hunting game in the woods back home, shot down Union soldiers like so many rabbits.

In a little grove of trees near Piney Flats, the story goes, three Union soldiers were ambushed by Confederates. When the smoke cleared, two soldiers lay dead and a third was gravely wounded. The sharpshooters moved on to other prey, leaving the wounded man to suffer all night, calling out piteously for someone to come help him. The sniper's minie ball had smashed through his right leg, severing an artery. The man ripped his shirt and applied a makeshift tourniquet, but the bleeding wouldn't stop. No one answered his calls for help, and by morning he was dead.

Several days later, the three bodies were discovered by neighborhood boys, who ran home to tell their parents of the grisly find. The dead soldiers were given a decent Christian burial, and the incident was soon forgotten.

A year later, a traveling sutler was passing the grove when he heard someone crying out for help. Not knowing about the ambush and the wounded soldier, he walked over to the trees to see if he could help. No one was there, but the sutler could still hear the voice, loud and clear in the twilight.

"Where are you?" the sutler asked.

The voice stopped. Nothing could be heard except the gentle rustling of the cold November wind.

The sutler decided that he must have been hearing things and continued on his way toward Piney Flats. When he arrived at the local tavern, he rounded up a friend to help him pop the cork from a fresh jug of liquor. A short time later, when both men were mellow, the sutler told his friend about the voice he had heard in the grove of trees. His companion suddenly grew silent.

"What's the matter?" the sutler asked.

"There was three Yankees killed up there about a year ago," his friend replied. "We found 'em a couple of days later, and we figure that one of 'em suffered some before he died, judgin' from the expression on his face. It might be his ghost that you heard."

It was the sutler's turn to fall silent. Then his friend, warm with fresh corn liquor, ventured a suggestion: "Why don't we ride up there and have a look?"

The sutler agreed, and his companion saddled two of his best horses. A half-hour later, jug still in hand, the two men stood next to the little grove of trees.

"I don't hear nothing," the friend said.

"Neither do I," replied the sutler, suddenly very nervous. "Let's go back. I suspect it's close to midnight, and I have to be on the road early in the morning."

As they turned to go, a voice behind them cried out, "Help me, help me! I'm bleedin' to death."

The sutler and his friend turned around. No one was in sight. "Help me, help me!" the voice called out again.

"It's coming from behind that boulder," the sutler said.

The two men crept to the rock and peered over. A soldier in a Union uniform lay on the ground holding his leg and trying to stop the bleeding. He looked real enough. And his predicament didn't seem far-fetched—after all, the war was still on. But just then, the soldier turned his head toward the sutler and his friend and grinned. His eyes were a glowing red.

The sutler headed at top speed in the opposite direction from Piney Flats, and without benefit of the horse he rode in on. He was never seen in that part of the country again.

His friend, who had more presence of mind, jumped on his horse and hurried back to town. When he returned to the tavern, he told everyone about the incident at the grove of trees. A group of curious townspeople visited the grove that very night, but no one saw or heard a thing. The consensus was that the sutler and his friend were merely suffering from a bad case of the "corn jitters."

But as in all stories of this sort, there exists a seed of plausibility. There *really was* a running Civil War skirmish through the area, and a few unlucky Yankee soldiers could easily have met their death in the little grove.

The copse is now part of a private farm, and the owner has posted No Trespassing signs around his property. But stern warnings do not deter those bent on derring-do. Today, when local boys get together to test their manhood, they goad each other into spending the night in the haunted copse near Piney Flats. Some gather enough courage to do so. Voices have been reported there over the years, but so far no one has seen the wounded soldier since that night so long ago when the sutler and his friend stared into the horrible red eyes of the ghost who cried for help.

Motifs: E 334.5. Ghost of soldier haunts battlefield; E 402.1.1.1.1. Ghost calls; E 337.2. Reenactment of tragedy seen; E 421.3. Luminous ghosts.

THE
GHOST LIGHT
OF MASTER'S KNOB

When Jim Oler was discharged from the army in 1955, the first thing he did was visit the old site of Troutmantown, now part of Johnson City, to relive a part of his youth. After climbing a hill known as Master's Knob, he gazed over a little hollow, straining his eyes to see if the ruins of a log cabin were still there. The building was nestled among the trees, its roof caved in.

"I was about twenty-two years old at the time," Oler said. "And I went down there to see if the lights were still there. But I had to get someone to go with me because I was scared to go there by myself."

The sky was streaked with the red and pink clouds of dusk. Oler and his companion looked again to the valley, straining their eyes. When darkness fell, a light suddenly appeared on a path a short distance from the ruined cabin. Slowly, it advanced toward the cabin, swinging back and forth as if someone were carrying it. When the light arrived at the ruins, it winked out. A few minutes later, it reappeared at its original spot on the path, followed the same route to the cabin, and once again went out.

Oler had seen the famous ghost light many times before. Indeed, it was part of his family lore. He was ten or twelve years old when he first pestered his father into taking him to see it. That night, as the pair sat atop Master's Knob looking down into the hollow and watching the light in horror and fascination, his father told him the story of the Civil War veteran who once lived in the cabin.

The man was a recluse, Oler's father told him. He didn't care to mix with his neighbors, and his neighbors considered him odd and didn't want to have anything to do with him. For many years, the old veteran lived alone in the cabin, venturing into town only infrequently. He had a reputation as a dangerous man, and most people gave him a wide berth.

Fearless neighborhood youths, on the other hand, liked to taunt him. Late at night, they would creep up to his cabin and throw rocks at it. The old veteran would burst through the front door brandishing his Enfield rifle and screaming curses into the night air. The boys would laugh and run into the woods, only to return the next night to taunt the man again.

In the winter of 1880, the veteran was found lying on the path leading to his cabin—frozen to death. The lantern he had been carrying was still lit. Soon afterward, the ghost light began to appear.

The story of the old veteran's death and the ghost light developed into a local legend. The curious came from far and wide to climb Master's Knob each evening after dark and watch the strange glow travel slowly up the path to the cabin before vanishing.

Jim Oler recalled his impressions from when he witnessed the light for the first time with his father. "We sat on the north slope of the ravine and, looking across a little stream, watched the spot where the body of the veteran was supposed to have been found," he said. "And sure enough, the light would appear, and it would look exactly like someone was walking, swinging a lantern. But it wasn't a yellow light. There was a bluish tint to it. And it would head toward the veteran's cabin, turn to the right, go up to the ruins of the cabin, then disappear.

"The area had a perfect atmosphere for a ghost story. Practically every time you went out, the light would appear. Even on hazy nights, when you couldn't even see the mountain across the hollow, you could see the light or the glow from it through the fog or haze or what have you.

"Back in those days, after the sun went down, it was so dark back there in the hollow that you could barely see your hand in front of your face. People were actually afraid to go through there. It was a spooky place, especially with that ghost-light story hanging over it."

The ghost light of Master's Knob was at the center of a practical joke engineered by Oler's father, James, and his Uncle Ben in the late 1930s. The joke was perpetrated on two small boys from the neighborhood, the Krenmans. Unfortunately for everyone concerned, the joke backfired.

James Oler and his brother were avid fox hunters. The Krenman boys pestered them so mercilessly about taking them hunting that the men finally agreed, but promised themselves that the boys would pay a heavy price for their persistence.

One night, a group of five fox hunters and the Krenman boys built a fire on Master's Knob and prepared to bed down for the night. They ate supper in the open air, which sharpened everyone's appetite. Before long, the entire party was pleasantly full. James Oler excused himself, and Uncle Ben and the other hunters—all of whom were in on the plot—sat down with the two boys. Uncle Ben told the story about the Civil War veteran and the ghost light. Then he pointed down into the valley, and sure enough, the ghost light was making its way up the path toward the cabin. But instead of adhering to the facts about the ghost light, Uncle Ben embellished the story. He told the wide-eyed Krenman boys that the ghost had been known to spring suddenly from the woods, especially when a campfire was burning.

The word *campfire* was the signal for James Oler to step out of the shadows with a blanket over his head, moaning piteously and holding a lantern beneath his costume to cast an eerie glow.

"Oh my God!" Uncle Ben shouted excitedly, pointing to the approaching apparition. "Look!"

The boys whirled around in time to see the ghostly James Oler and his lantern. Panic-stricken, the Krenmans jumped up and ran toward a steep bluff, dragging Uncle Ben with them—dragging him so vigorously, in fact, that he tripped and broke his ankle. Uncle Ben and the boys went over the bluff and began rolling downhill toward the valley of the ghost light.

Meanwhile, the hunting dogs were beside themselves with excitement. Two of them tried to go around one side of a tree while the hunter holding them went around the other, which snapped the tether. Suddenly, all the dogs took a notion to race across the hill. One of them was never seen again. The commotion scared James Oler so badly that he thought the real ghost of the Civil War veteran was actually in the camp. He dropped his lantern and took off running, his blanket flapping behind him.

When they rolled to a stop at the bottom of the bluff, the Krenman boys scrambled to their feet and started running for home, four miles distant. They leaped into bed with their parents and refused to budge the rest of the night. The hunters spent the evening gathering up dogs, rifles, and other personal effects that had been scattered in the panic. Then they took Uncle Ben to a doctor so his ankle could be set.

The next day, James Oler and Uncle Ben met the Krenman boys on the streets of Johnson City. Uncle Ben's lower leg was in a splint, but he was hobbling around well considering that his ankle was nearly the size of a watermelon.

Uncle Ben hailed the Krenmans. "What happened to you fellers last night?" he asked. "You took off so fast we didn't get a chance to say good-bye."

The Krenman boys smiled sheepishly.

"I can't say I much blame you for running off like that," James Oler added. "I'll admit it was pretty scary with that thing jumping out of the woods and all."

"Aw, come on, Mr. Oler," one of the boys said. "We knowed it was you all along."

"I suspect you're right, boys. But this should teach you not to pester grown folks all the time about going hunting. You never know what they might do to get back at you. I suspect you've learned your lesson. You ain't never going to live this down—especially since you broke poor Ben's ankle here, and lost one of my best dogs to boot."

According to Jim Oler, his father and his Uncle Ben were as good as their word. "They told that story on those two guys for the rest of their lives," he said.

Motifs: E 530.1. Ghostlike lights; E 599.7. Ghost carries lantern; E 334. Non-malevolent ghost haunts spot where tragedy occurred; K 1665.* The trickster injures himself while tricking another; K 1682.1(g). Scarer discomfited; K 1682.1. "Big 'Fraid and Little 'Fraid." Trickster disguised as ghost attempts to scare others, is scared himself.

THE
STRANGE CASE
OF KATY FISHER

When an electrical storm strikes the mountains, the violence of wind and rain can be overpowering. Thunder ricochets off mountains and rumbles through hollows. Strange objects are often carried by the gale—the wind is blamed for transporting things aloft and carrying them over many miles of open country.

More than a century ago, in a small community just north of the town of Hampton, the wind from a summer electrical storm was said to have deposited a strange young woman unceremoniously in front of a farmer's house. Those involved in the incident could offer no more plausible explanation for her sudden appearance. When Frank Hyder discovered the woman on his front porch, it marked the beginning of one of the oddest tales ever to emerge from upper East Tennessee.

The storm-blown, sodden woman had no idea who she was or how she had gotten to Hyder's five-hundred-acre farm. Hyder contacted the Carter County sheriff. The authorities tried to learn the young woman's identity, but all efforts failed. She carried no baggage or identification. She could not remember her name. The Hyders generously welcomed her into their home as a member of their large and bustling family. They decided to call her "Katy Fisher."

People in the neighborhood came to the Hyder farm to gawk at the odd visitor. The word *witch* was even used to describe her. The young woman was shy, and the attention bothered her considerably. Frank Hyder tried to protect her. Luckily for both Katy and Frank, the novelty of her arrival soon wore off, and life at the Hyder farm returned to normal.

According to all reports, Katy adapted well to the vigorous life of a large farm. She was a strapping girl who could lift objects that were usually beyond the strength of a woman. Yet for all her strength, she was amazingly gentle and feminine. She had a rapport with animals that was almost supernatural. For example, it was said that cows would come to her when she called their names. Everyone who knew Katy came to love her and understand her loneliness. The Hyders were like family to her, but she always longed to know just who her real family was. Without that knowledge, she could never lead a completely normal life.

Around Hampton, stories about Katy continue to be told. One story concerns her star-crossed love affair with Jeremiah Torrence. In the 1880s, the Torrence family owned a large tract of local land. They were successful farmers. Jeremiah was the oldest son of the family, about twenty-three when he met Katy. He was well-hewn and unusually handsome and intelligent. Katy was immediately taken with him, but her shyness initially kept them from growing close. Jeremiah, it turned out, was just as taken with her.

One night at a community dance, Jeremiah and Katy sat across the hall from each other. They exchanged gazes, but Jeremiah couldn't gather the nerve to make a move. The stalemate lasted almost an hour. Finally, he took the plunge and crossed the hall to where Katy was sitting. When he asked her to dance, she readily consented, to his delight. The song over, Jeremiah asked her for another dance, and she agreed again. That was all it took to set tongues to wagging. People noticed that Katy and Jeremiah didn't dance with anyone else the rest of the night—they didn't even look at anyone else. Frank

Hyder asked Katy how she felt about Jeremiah, but she would say nothing, and he wisely did not push the subject any further.

In the days and weeks that followed, Katy became even more remote than was her custom. She would leave the house after the supper dishes were done, disappear for hours, then return late at night. Sometimes, Frank Hyder would find her standing by the corncrib, gazing over the fields and mountains with a glassy look in her eye. Other times, she would climb up into the hayloft and sit for hours humming to herself. She would sing a little song about a lady who had left her husband—a carpenter—for a rich man, only to find out too late that she had made a mistake. Katy seemed to find an odd comfort in that song, and she sang it often. Neither Frank nor anyone else in Carter County had taught it to her:

"Well met, well met, my own true love.
Well met, well met," cried he.
"For I have returned from the salt, salt sea,
All for the love of thee."

Jeremiah courted Katy regularly and well. But the more he tried to win her, the more remote she became. She was not unkind to him— she just seemed to prefer her own company. At first, Jeremiah could not understand her attitude. He was not without wealth. He was also considered handsome by the girls in town. And Katy did not seem to have any other love interest. So why was she so unresponsive? When he finally discovered Katy's true nature, it frightened him badly.

One day in April, Jeremiah was out plowing a field. The temperature was warm for that time of year, and the hard work had made him hot and sweaty. He stopped plowing for a moment, removed his hat to wipe his brow, then chanced to glance across the field. A distant figure was making its way across the meadow, heading in the general direction of Doe Creek. It was Katy. Jeremiah tried to hail her, but there was no reply.

Tying his mule to the nearest fence post, he took off across the field after her, catching her at the edge of the woods. He hailed her again, but she still didn't answer. Her eyes seemed to be fixed on an object somewhere ahead, in the thick forest. Jeremiah stepped in front of her path to get her attention. She stopped but did not acknowledge his presence, gazing steadfastly ahead, as if in a trance. Frustrated and confused, Jeremiah stepped aside and let her pass. She disappeared into the woods.

The next day, Jeremiah again met Katy. This time, she smiled and asked him how he was. He asked her what had happened and why she had ignored him.

"I don't know," she replied. "I don't remember seeing you yesterday."

"But I was right in front of you!" Jeremiah protested. "I spoke to you. I even yelled to get your attention."

Katy smiled. "You probably did," she answered. "Things like this happen to me once in a while. People will say they've seen me in certain places, and I won't remember. Then they'll say they spoke to me, and I won't remember that, either."

Jeremiah didn't understand. In fact, not even the best doctors of his time would have understood. Today, psychiatrists would recognize Katy's episodes as a fugue state. Pressures can build up to such a level that a person's mind goes blank, causing a type of amnesia. During a fugue, victims remember nothing of the past. Many do not even know their names. The victim assumes a different personality during the fugue and actually lives another life. Traditional reality vanishes and is replaced with another kind of reality, the product of a mind desperately reaching for escape from past problems. The affliction may continue for years, until the brain suddenly "snaps back" and the victim reverts to the old self, remembering nothing of the time in the fugue state.

Psychiatrists today would be able to help Katy. They would probably be able to discover who she really was and where she had come from. But in the 1880s, there was no such thing as a psychiatrist— Sigmund Freud was an ocean away just beginning to formulate his theories on human behavior. The deeply religious people of Carter County believed that Satan was behind all mental illness.

If Katy Fisher really suffered from a fugue, she never snapped out of it. And she never married Jeremiah Torrence. Katy told him that she loved him but thought it best if they never saw each other again. Jeremiah could not deal with Katy's spells, and he probably would have ended the affair himself if Katy hadn't done so. A short time later, he married a girl from Greeneville, but he never forgot Katy.

Katy lived out her life on the Hyder farm, never managing to uncover her past. She grew even more reclusive. As the years passed, she spoke less and sang more—mostly to herself. She never married and died an old woman, still being called by the name the Hyders had given her. Today, nestled in the Hyder family plot, there stands a tombstone with the name "Katy Fisher" chiseled on it, a lasting memorial to a tragic woman with no name and no memories who is said to have blown in on the wind over a century ago.

Motifs: D 2135. Magic air journey; D 2000. Magic forgetfulness; J 2012. Person does not know himself; F 900. Extraordinary occurrences; D 2121. Magic journey; D 2137. Natural law suspended.

THE
PHANTOM
HORSEMAN

Ghosts do not seem to care whether the places they haunt have been touched by civilization—in the city or out in the country, it makes no difference to them. It does, however, make a difference to the living. Experiencing an eerie haunt in a remote area, where the nearest neighbor may live miles away, can be quite unnerving.

James Blevins was only sixteen when he and several other young men were hired to "grub" at a remote, recently purchased farmhouse near Elizabethton in the 1920s. Their job was to clear fields of scrub trees and underbrush, a task they contracted to do for fifty cents a day. Late one afternoon, the boys arrived at the property on horse-back and installed their animals in a ramshackle old barn behind the farmhouse. The two-story white clapboard farmhouse was empty, and the boys planned to stay there during the time they worked.

The old farmhouse was a handsome building featuring a long, railed porch that ran along its front and side. There was nothing particularly forbidding about the structure, even though the house was in a state of disrepair. Some of the windows were broken, paint was peeling from the clapboards, and some of the wood was starting to rot. The owner planned to improve the property and rent it to another farmer.

The land surrounding the house had a number of good fields and meadows. About three hundred feet from the house was a brook that gurgled down the mountainside, its waters well-stocked with trout and other fish. The woods teemed with squirrels and rabbits.

The front porch allowed an unimpeded view of mountains and forests. On the first night, as the boys sat on the front steps and watched a blazing sunset behind the mountains, they were struck with the beauty of the view. All in all, the house and its environs were pleasant enough. The boys expected to spend a few uneventful days cleaning out brush, then return home.

Settling in for the night, they built a small fire in the fireplace and cooked their supper. After eating, they spread their pallets on the floor and sat around talking, planning the next day's work, and gossiping for a while before retiring. Soon, James Blevins and his friends were fast asleep, lulled by the crackling of the fire and the cheerful sound of crickets outside the house.

Then, sometime during the night, the boys were awakened by the sound of a horse slowly coming up the path toward the house. It was snorting and blowing, as if the trip up the mountain had completely exhausted it. When the horse arrived in front of the house, they heard it stop. Someone got off and threw his saddle on the porch. The boys assumed that the owner of the house had decided to visit the property and oversee the clearing of the land.

After what would have been enough time for the rider to put his horse in the barn, they heard the back door of the house squeak open and footsteps come down the hallway and ascend the steps, and then the boys heard the sharp sound of an upstairs door slamming. They thought it odd that the owner had not checked in with them first. Suddenly, the thought struck them that the rider might be someone other than the owner—possibly a dangerous intruder.

Young Blevins decided that he would light a coal-oil lantern, walk upstairs, and see if the visitor was actually the owner. He had brought a shotgun to kill fresh meat, so he reached for the weapon and loaded it just in case. Next, he and a couple of the other boys climbed the stairs and checked the rooms on the second floor. To their surprise, the rooms were empty. They returned to the first floor, walked out the front door, and checked the porch, where they had heard the saddle thrown down. They found nothing.

Then, from inside the house, they heard the sound of someone wearing heavy boots walking down the stairs—the stairs they had just come down themselves! Again, a quick investigation proved that no one was there.

The boys were thoroughly spooked by now. Since it was too dangerous to return home over the mountain path in the dark, they voted to stay on the property—but not in the house—until daylight. They moved their pallets into the front yard and spent the rest of the night in the company of the crickets and lightning bugs.

When the early-morning light finally streaked the sky, the boys loaded up their horses and snaked their way down the treacherous mountain path. In Elizabethton, they unloaded their unused provisions and equipment. Then they located the owner of the house.

"Did you ride up to the house last night?" Blevins asked him, thinking perhaps that the man had been playing a practical joke.

"No, I didn't," the man replied. He paused for a moment, a funny look in his eye. "Why?" he asked. "What happened?"

The boys told him about the ghostly horse and rider and the mysterious footsteps walking up to the second floor of the farmhouse. They also told him that he would have to find someone else to clear the land, because they were not going to return to the house.

The owner listened patiently to the boys' story, then confessed that he had acquired the property from a widow whose husband had recently died. The late husband had inherited the land from his father, who in turn had inherited it from *his* father. The late husband's great-grandfather had been the owner of one of the original North Carolina land grants, issued long before Tennessee became a state. Just before the husband died, he had made his wife promise that she would never sell the property. But the wife, strapped financially and unwilling to stay in a house located miles from nowhere, had sold it anyway. Then she'd moved out of the farmhouse to live with her children.

The widow had told the present owner that on the night before she was to leave the house forever, as she was in her bedroom preparing to go to sleep, she, too, had heard a horse come up the mountain path and halt in front of the house. Then she heard footsteps come up the stairs and stop at the closed door of her room. She first thought that her son, who was helping her move, had come to the house unexpectedly. But when the door opened, she was horrified to see the apparition of her dead husband standing in the doorway, scowling at her. Her impression was that the ghost of her husband had returned to let her know, in no uncertain terms, just how unhappy he was that she had sold the house. The apparition soon disappeared. The woman fled the house in terror and stayed in the barn for the rest of the night, until her son came for her the next morning.

"I guess that was his ghost you heard," the owner told young Blevins and his friends. "I've heard things about former owners coming back to protect their property. I reckon that old man haunts that house and I'm stuck with his ghost. I reckon I'm going to have one heck of a time trying to rent the place now!"

Motifs: E 279.2. Ghost disturbs sleeping person; E 423.1.3.5. Actions of ghostly horse; E 402. Mysterious ghostlike noises are heard; cf. E 402(d). Ghostlike noises cause owner to abandon farm; E 338. Non-malevolent ghost haunts building.

THE
ADVENTURES
OF THE
HAUNTED GUN

In some upper East Tennessee families, it is a practice to destroy favorite personal objects belonging to the dead, for fear they might attract the ghost of the deceased. Sometimes, a ghost will return to haunt those who inherited its former possessions, much as a ghost haunts a house it owned before death. Such occurrences are known as "manabee" hauntings.

Around the turn of this century, a manabee came into the lives of a family from Erwin, in Unicoi County. The story began when a young male member of the family purchased a pistol from a man in North Carolina. Soon after he bought the gun, the young man and his girlfriend attended a Sunday-night prayer meeting at a small Baptist church in Paul's Gap. For some reason, the young man took the pistol with him to church.

After the meeting, the two were returning home when a strange man suddenly appeared, walking on the opposite side of the woman from the young man. Neither one knew where the stranger had come from, but they assumed he had been to the prayer meeting and was returning home.

At that time, traveling in Unicoi County after dark could be dangerous. Wild animals were still abundant, and bear attacks were not uncommon. The young man was at first pleased that the stranger seemed to be offering extra protection for him and his girlfriend. Then the couple noticed something odd about the stranger—he said absolutely nothing. In fact, he did not even acknowledge their presence. Furthermore, he mimicked all their movements. When they stopped, he stopped. When they started walking again, so did he. The stranger's actions were so unusual that the pair became uneasy. The young man felt it necessary to reach into his pocket and wrap his hand around the pistol, just in case he was forced to use it.

The young man finally saw his girlfriend to her house. When he turned around, the stranger had vanished. He searched the vicinity, fearing the stranger was waiting in the bushes to attack the girl or her parents as soon as he left. But he was nowhere to be found, and the young man could only assume he had continued on his way and that everything was all right.

A short time later, the young man reached his home. He shared a small log house with his brother, both of them sleeping in the same bed. That night, after the young man's brother set the bolt on their door, they climbed into the bed. Just then, the door opened and the manabee appeared. He walked through the doorway and then disappeared.

After the initial shock of the manabee's appearance wore off, the young man accused his brother of failing to lock the door. He scrambled out of the bed and reset the lock himself. It was not very long before the door opened again and the manabee walked in.

The young man spoke to him. "Who are you?" he asked. "And what do you want?"

The manabee said nothing.

The young man had stashed the pistol in the pocket of his overalls, and he threatened to shoot the intruder unless he answered immediately. Still, the stranger said nothing. The young man drew the pistol and shot once. The manabee disappeared in a cloud of blue powder smoke.

The brothers fastened the door for a third time and climbed back into the bed. And for the third time, the door to the cabin opened and the manabee walked in. Now totally frightened, the young man drew his pistol and shot two or three times at the manabee, who once again disappeared.

The brothers were so shaken by their experience that they stayed up the rest of the night. As they talked about the ghost, they concluded that it was somehow connected with the gun. And since the ghost seemed harmless enough, they decided to have a little fun with their manabee.

"Back in those days," remembered Guard Banner, a cousin of the two brothers, "boys from surroundin' communities would come to Erwin to visit their girlfriends. Other boys who didn't have girlfriends at the time would 'rock' the couples as the boys took the girls home. They wouldn't try to hit them with the rocks, but they would throw close enough that the girls would scream and run."

One night, the local boys chose the wrong person to pick on—the young man who owned the pistol. "There were some old grapevines growin' across a wagon road," Guard Banner said, "and some of the boys got on top of those grapevines waitin' to 'rock' my cousin when he walked by. And several of the boys were also hidden in the bushes alongside the road."

But Banner's cousin, feeling something was up, had earlier made sure that one of the local boys borrowed his haunted pistol, so the manabee was certain to pay the rock throwers a visit. "So this man come down the road," Guard Banner said, "and walked a little past where those boys were layin' up in the grapevines. Then he turned around and walked under them again, as if he was searchin' for somethin'. The boys spoke to him—told him to get out of the way so they could have a clear shot with their rocks—but he just stood still and said nothing. Finally, one of the boys said, 'Now, if you don't speak to us and tell us what you want, we're going to shoot down here on you.'"

Again the manabee said nothing. The boy who had the pistol fired a shot. "When the smoke cleared out," Banner said, "they could see that he was still a-standin' there. They shot again, the smoke cleared away, and he was still a-standin' there. Well, the boys couldn't take it no longer, and, buddy, they came out of them grapevines and hit the ground a-runnin'."

A short time later, the young man sold the gun to Banner's father, Henry, who was well aware of the manabee haunting it. "My mother wouldn't let him take the gun into the house with him," Guard Banner said. "So he'd leave it in the blacksmith shop because my mother didn't want no parts of it."

One day, the Unicoi County sheriff and his wife joined Banner's family to make apple butter. When they finally finished stirring the apple butter and pouring it into jars, it was late and nearly dark. The sheriff turned to Banner's father and said, "Henry, let me have your gun. I didn't bring mine with me tonight. I left it at the house."

Henry Banner agreed and walked out to his blacksmith shop and picked up the gun. But he didn't tell the sheriff about the manabee that was certain to visit.

The next morning about daylight, Banner's father spied the sheriff walking briskly up the road with the gun in his hand. Henry Banner met his friend on the front porch.

"I knew that there was a gun like this around here somewhere, Henry, but I didn't know you had the darned thing," the sheriff hissed between clenched teeth.

"Why, sheriff," Henry asked nonchalantly, "is there something wrong?"

"You're darn right there's something wrong!" the sheriff answered angrily. "Me and my wife started down the road from your place last night and this man come to us. He didn't say a word. He just walked alongside. I tried to talk to him but he wouldn't answer. My wife was so scared she was clingin' to me like a vine. But I couldn't arrest him or nothin', because he wasn't doin' anything wrong—just walkin' alongside us. Well, we got to the house and this man walked right inside. Then he disappeared. We locked the door, but it kept comin' unlatched and this man kept comin' in. I'd threaten him and he'd disappear. We couldn't keep the door fastened. Finally, I figured out that the gun was causin' all this, and I went out and laid it on the back porch."

Then the sheriff pointed the pistol at the elder Banner, shaking it angrily. "So there it is back, Henry. I don't want no more to do with that gun. My wife and I ain't slept a wink all night."

Sometime after the incident with the sheriff, Henry Banner was working for the federal government, building a fish hatchery. One of the other workers at the hatchery eyed Henry's gun and offered to trade two pigs for the pistol. Henry agreed, and the trade was made the next day.

The day after the trade, the man was back, mumbling something about a door that wouldn't stay latched and a strange man who kept coming inside. "I want to sell that pistol back to you, Henry," he said.

"Don't need it," Henry replied. "Already got a shotgun. Don't need a pistol."

"Look," the man said. "Tell you what I'll do. I'll give you back this pistol, let you keep the pigs, plus a dollar on each one of them pigs."

"Done," Henry said quickly.

"My daddy had bought those pigs at six weeks old," Guard Banner said. "The man must have really wanted to get rid of that pistol bad."

A week later, Guard Banner sold the pistol to a traveling salesman who was headed to California. And that was the last that anyone ever saw of the haunted gun and the manabee that went with it.

Motifs: E 332.2. Person meets ghost on road; E 338.1(c). Ghost opens doors and windows repeatedly; E 419.10. Concern of ghost about belongings of its lifetime; E 235.3(c). Boys raise ghost as a lark, are scared by the ghost; E 332.2(f). Ghost walks with traveler in silence.

THE
HAUNTED
THEATER

I have been cautioned that, as a folklorist, I should never inject myself into any story that I've collected. But on the other hand, it is seldom that a folklorist is privileged to experience firsthand the legend that he is writing about. There is a certain amount of comfort in knowing that at least one of the stories I have recorded is solidly based in fact. Therefore, I will tell of a personal experience with a haunting, encountered on the grounds of the Veterans Affairs Medical Center at Mountain Home in Johnson City.

Mountain Home is filled with violent memories of traumatic events. Many veterans hospitals, especially the ones with domiciliaries, have that sinister aura about them. Death permeates the air because death is such a part of domiciliary life. I myself have spent time in the "dom" recovering from an illness and can attest to that fact. Many people come to the domiciliary to die—those with terminal illnesses who must live out the rest of their short lives under medical supervision. From this sullen ambiance, ghost stories are very likely to spring.

To hear veterans tell it, Mountain Home is filled with ghosts. Nearly every building on the hospital grounds has its resident spirit.

Of course, the Department of Veterans Affairs denies any knowledge of supernatural activity. The government is not in the business of perpetuating ghost stories, and most inquiries are met with silence. But the ghostly traditions persist.

One oft-told tale at Mountain Home concerns an old soldier, dressed in a Spanish-American War uniform complete with campaign hat, who walks along the maze of roads on the hospital grounds. Observers have no doubt that this vision is a real ghost—the specter's feet never touch the pavement!

Another strange story from Mountain Home is that of the drenched apparition of a former patient who stalks the banks of the fishpond, located in a little valley below the hospital, beside the railroad tracks. Twenty years ago, the man drowned in that pond, and his shade is said to appear on each anniversary of the tragedy.

A third legend deals with the mysterious crying of a young child near the administration building of the James H. Quillen School of Medicine, located on the hospital grounds. The wailing is said to come from the ghost of a little boy—the son of a former hospital director—who drowned many years ago.

The plethora of ghost stories from Mountain Home is due, in part, to the age of the complex. Built around 1903 for army veterans who fought for the North during the Civil War, and originally called the Mountain Branch of the National Home for Disabled Volunteer Soldiers, Mountain Home has taken into its care untold thousands of men and has provided for them until they died.

Mountain Home came about as the result of a forty-year-old dream of President Abraham Lincoln. During his presidency, Lincoln enjoyed the company of war veterans and spent much of his time at the Old Soldiers Home in Washington. He hoped that a grateful nation would provide for the welfare of Civil War veterans after the peace had been signed. His hope to build a national soldiers' home in the South was based upon the fact that an estimated one-fourth of the two million Union soldiers came from below the Mason-Dixon line. Lincoln was assassinated before he could start building his dream of a national network of soldiers' homes, but others eventually carried on his work at Mountain Home.

Those who designed Mountain Home were farsighted when they provided a first-class theater for the veterans. Memorial Hall is said to have been patterned after the St. James Theater in New York City, and today remains a classic example of a turn-of-the-century opera house. It is also said to be the most haunted building at Mountain Home.

Built in 1904, Memorial Hall is a stunning example of Beaux-Arts architecture as practiced by J. H. Freelander, a student of the famous architect Stanford White. To the eye, the theater is an aesthetic feast. The jewel in Memorial Hall's crown is its grand circular staircase, which ascends to the balcony in a great red arc and descends to the opposite side of the lobby. The main floor slopes toward a raised stage and orchestra pit, where the Mountain Home military band used to play twice-weekly concerts and accompany silent movies in the early decades of this century. Upstairs are a balcony and a row of three private boxes on each side of the auditorium. Behind the balcony is a large projection booth.

One story about Memorial Hall's ghosts sprang up within the ranks of local thespians, who until recently used the auditorium to stage plays. They found that if a person seats himself in the little half-basement under the stage and remains quiet, unseen phantoms can be heard treading the boards overhead. A variation of the same story was told to me by an old-timer who claimed that he had heard a single pair of footsteps walk from one end of the stage to the other and back again. He had been alone in the theater late one night, working on some props in the half-basement. When he climbed up to the stage to see who was there, he found the stage—as well as the entire theater—empty. The old-timer immediately walked out of the theater and swore that he would never work there again at night alone.

For two years, I was the projectionist at Memorial Hall. During my tenure, I had ample opportunity to be alone in the late-night silence of the cavernous theater. On occasion, I stood in absolute silence and listened for the ghostly footsteps. The theater can play tricks on the senses. Even with the house lights on, deep shadows pervade crevices and corners of the building. The ancient wood superstructure creaks and groans, especially in cold weather. It was easy to see how someone could be misled into believing that ghosts haunt Memorial Hall. But I secretly wished the stories I had heard about the place were true. Then one night, during the first part of my second year at Memorial Hall, I finally got my wish.

To set up the theater to show a film, it was necessary to wheel the loudspeaker, housed in a giant black box and stored backstage, to a position to the rear of the screen and connect it to a large jack in the stage floor. Each night after the show was over, I had to return to the stage, disconnect the speaker, and wheel it back to its storage place. One night, I showed a double-feature western, and the hour for quitting was quite late. After shutting down the projection booth, I walked backstage. It was nearly dark, and only the glow of the house lights penetrated the myriad tiny sound holes in the screen. Backstage was bathed in a spooky half-light.

I had just reached down to unhook the speaker jack from the stage floor when I heard breathing behind me. I looked around and saw a figure. Then I recognized it. The face was that of the former projectionist, a patient who had died suddenly of a heart attack. It was the man I had replaced the year before. I didn't have time to regain my senses because, in a flash, the apparition vanished.

My predecessor, the former projectionist, had been dead only a few months, so he could not have been responsible for all the other ghost stories about Memorial Hall. From that moment, I was more inclined to believe that some of those older stories just might have a basis in fact. And after that night, I always waited until the next morning to disconnect the speaker cables.

Motifs: E 402.1.2. Footsteps of invisible ghost heard; E 402.1. Noises presumably caused by ghost of person; E 338. Non-malevolent ghost haunts building.

THE
GHOSTS
OF ETSU

It's a shame that East Tennessee State University, located on the west slope of the Appalachian Mountains in Johnson City, does not offer a major in parapsychology. The campus is absolutely infested with ghosts, ghoulies, and things that go bump in the night. Its massive brick buildings are lonely and spooky at night, especially after students have left for the day and the custodians are working alone in gloomy hallways. Silence permeates, deep shadows throw corners into a kind of translucent darkness, and a person can imagine almost anything is lurking there, ready to spring.

Gilbreath Hall hosts one of ETSU's most famous ghosts. Maintenance personnel who clean the building after hours and student workers who man the computer labs until two in the morning can testify to that fact. They will tell you that the wispy culprit is none other than Sidney Gilbreath himself.

Gilbreath was the first president of East Tennessee State Normal School, the name under which East Tennessee State University opened in 1911. He was a wunderkind in turn-of-the-century Tennessee public education. He became Tennessee state superintendent of public schools at age twenty-six, still the youngest ever to hold that position. He was also a school superintendent in Monroe County, a president of Hiwassee College, a professor at Peabody College, and the superintendent of public schools in Chattanooga. Gilbreath campaigned diligently to be president of the new normal school in Johnson City, and he was considered a shoo-in for the post when the school began operations.

"Uncle Sid," as he was known, was a strait-laced individual with a puritanical streak. His tenure as president of the normal school was stormy, and his moral code—especially the part of it designed to ensure the virtuous behavior of all coeds—spawned a host of anecdotes and legends. For instance, any female student riding in an automobile with a male unfamiliar to Gilbreath risked expulsion from the institution. There was no malice intended by Gilbreath's unbendable regulations. He simply believed that education was important business. And he was as stubborn and passionate about his rules as the shock of red hair on top of his head would suggest.

When he wasn't acting as chaperon, Uncle Sid was busy fighting the Tennessee legislature, some members of which seemed bent on interfering with the normal school's financial workings. He also made some bitter enemies among members of the charter faculty at the school. In the early 1920s, they attempted to dethrone him by fabricating a sex scandal. Gilbreath was accused of dallying with one of the maids in Carter Hall, the women's dormitory, but he was acquitted of all charges. All in all, Gilbreath's ten years as president of the normal school had their ups and downs, but the school grew steadily during his tenure.

The original administration building on the campus was named Gilbreath Hall. It is said that Uncle Sid selected the site by walking to the edge of a rolling field and jamming a wooden stake into the ground. Today, Gilbreath Hall houses the Computer Science, Math, and Drama departments at East Tennessee State University. The building's architecture is plainly turn-of-the-century "American scholastic." Inside, high ceilings tell of a time when heating fuel was cheap. Old-fashioned wooden doors lead to large offices off the main hallways. Cast-iron lamps with old-fashioned globes decorate the steps outside the building. Very little of the "old" look of the building has been sacrificed, in spite of a general effort by the administration to update the architecture on campus.

Maintenance personnel say the ghost of Uncle Sid roams Gilbreath Hall, acting very much like a fussy custodian. When the lights go out as the janitors are leaving for the night, the slamming of windows and doors left open by mistake vibrates throughout the building. An approaching thunderstorm also prompts the closing of windows by an unseen hand. Apparently, the long-departed Gilbreath takes an active interest in the welfare of his building.

Late one night, the graduate dean was in his Gilbreath Hall office when he heard noises overhead. There was no one else in the building at the time, and he decided to see what was making the sounds. After walking upstairs, he couldn't find anything on the upper floor—but he still heard noises overhead. The dean decided to dismiss the whole incident and return to his office, but an unknown force tried to draw him back. The feeling was unmistakable and powerful, yet not malevolent. He resisted the call but could not forget the feeling.

The next day, he collared one of the maintenance men cleaning the building. "Is there an attic in this building?" the dean asked.

"Not that I know of," the custodian replied.

"Then how about a crawlspace? Something above the third floor of the building?"

"I really don't know," the janitor answered, "but let's find out."

The janitor got a ladder and found a trapdoor that led to an area between the third floor and the roof. And sure enough, there was a low-ceilinged attic there.

After the dean climbed into the little attic, he felt a powerful compulsion to look in one particular corner. He discovered two framed pictures. One was a big engraving of the Cherokee Indian Chief Mushuladubbe. The other was a huge photograph of Abraham Lincoln. Apparently, those two items had been removed from an office wall during the renovation of Gilbreath Hall and discarded in the attic. Just as the dean was picking up the photo of Lincoln, something brushed against his shoulder, and a voice whispered in his ear, "Thanks, from Uncle Sid."

The dean left the attic thinking that the ghost of Sidney Gilbreath roams the halls of the building, as it probably does. He could only surmise that Abraham Lincoln and Mushuladubbe must have been important figures in Gilbreath's mind. Perhaps the pictures had been removed from the walls of Gilbreath's office, and he wanted very much to save them.

Hundreds of other incidents suggest the presence of Uncle Sid in Gilbreath Hall, but actual sightings of his ghost are much harder to come by. It was a unique event when Terri Voyles of Bristol, a student at ETSU, saw the ghost of Uncle Sid from her room in Carter Hall.

"I stood at my window and looked across the campus," Voyles said. "There are windows at the top of Gilbreath Hall, in the attic. Suddenly, I saw a figure standing at one of those windows with what looked like a red light behind it. This was about two in the morning, and I was thinking about Uncle Sid at the time.

"Earlier in the evening, a friend of mine was appearing in a play in the theater in Gilbreath Hall. Between acts, he had to wash the makeup off his face. Suddenly, the water and lights went off. After a few minutes of searching for the trouble and finding none, my friend became very frustrated. Suddenly, he shouted, 'Damn it, Gilbreath, get the lights on and let me get my face washed!' And immediately the lights and water returned.

"This is the incident I was thinking of when I saw the figure in the attic window at Gilbreath Hall. Then I looked away for a second, looked back, and it was gone."

Gilbreath Hall is not the only spooky building on the ETSU campus. Mathes Hall lends a feeling of isolation, mainly because its interior layout is so fragmented. It would be impossible for a person to move quickly from one end of the building to the other in case of an emergency. The recital hall, located in the center, rises into the upper stories, thus cutting the building in half. In order to get from one part of the second floor to the other, it is necessary to go down one flight of steps, walk through more lonely hallways, and ascend another set of steps. Furthermore, sound seems to echo from one hallway to another, intensifying an already eerie effect. Custodians who clean Mathes Hall at night have acquired the habit of frequently looking over their shoulder, just to make sure that they are alone.

One custodian said that, on several occasions, she descended the steps of Mathes Hall and heard footsteps behind her. When she stopped, the footsteps stopped. When she started, the footsteps started again. One time, she turned on her heels and ran upstairs to see who was there. Of course, she saw nothing. However, she continued to feel that she was not being tailed by a ghost, but rather by someone playing a trick on her. "I ain't afraid of no boogers!" she declared.

But one night when she was least expecting it, something frightening happened in the building that made her doubt her bravery. On the second floor of Mathes Hall, there is a little cell-like room that houses janitorial supplies. It can also be used by the custodian as a place to rest. One night, the woman was sitting in her closet when she heard a tremendous crash overhead. The entire building shook with the impact. When she went to investigate, nothing was amiss.

A few minutes later, she heard the same ear-shattering noise again—a loud crash that sounded like part of the building was caving in. This time, she was terrified. She called a friend of hers on the telephone, and they talked until it was time for her to leave. Although the intensity of the sound overhead indicated that extensive damage might have been done to the building, none was ever found.

Sometimes, it is difficult to connect a particular ghost with a specific haunting at ETSU. Often, the most likely candidate for a haunting is chosen by a process of elimination, as in the case of Burleson Hall, the English building. A former professor of English, a highly respected Shakespearean scholar, is blamed by informed sources for the haunting of the building—a building named after her father.

Christine Burleson was connected with ETSU for most of her life. Daughter of charter faculty member David Sinclair Burleson, she was a high-school freshman when she started contributing to the normal school's student magazine, the *East Tennessee Teacher*. In the first issue of another school magazine, *Blue and Gold*, there is a photograph of her demurely posing with the rest of the school's girls' basketball team. Even in the ancient, fuzzy photo, her haunting and pensive beauty is apparent. In maturity, her features were described as striking.

"Miss Christine" graduated from a two-year program at the normal school in 1917 and attended the University of Tennessee. She earned her bachelor's degree at Vassar in 1920. Then she graduated from Columbia University with a master's degree and earned another master's from Oxford University in England. She taught English for many years at ETSU, especially courses in Shakespeare, and was honored with the Distinguished Faculty Award in 1967.

That is not to say she was universally loved among the faculty. Miss Christine was reserved with many of her colleagues. She wasn't particularly fond of most of the other English professors, even seeking to avoid some of them. She seemed to think the younger members of the department were upstarts. Miss Christine liked teaching Shakespeare so much that she felt she "owned" the subject at ETSU, and she grew resentful when others tried to enter her territory. She never married—some say because of a tragic love affair early in her life.

A horrible debilitating disease ran in Christine Burleson's family. Her mother had died of it. When Miss Christine was in her sixties, she, too, contracted the malady. Confined to a wheelchair, the independent-minded woman was determined that she would never be a burden to anyone. In the early 1970s, she put a bullet through her brain.

The ghost of Christine Burleson has been associated with a variety of activity in Burleson Hall, like the distinct sound of a woman's moaning that came from one faculty member's office for about a month in the fall of 1988. But the most tangible evidence that something unearthly inhabits Burleson Hall is a large photograph of David Sinclair Burleson, Miss Christine's father, on the second floor. It is one of those eerie photographs in which the eyes seem alive. No matter where you move in sight of the picture, the eyes follow you. According to campus tradition, the eyes in the photograph belong to Christine Burleson, and not to her father. The beauty of the eyes is not the kind normally associated with a male. One of the most striking physical attributes of Christine Burleson was her large, beautiful eyes.

Of all the ghostly traditions at East Tennessee State University, none is better documented than the screaming ghost of Cooper Hall. She has been the subject of newspaper articles and investigations by local historians. Some people think the ghost actually existed, but others think she was the result of sophomoric pranks played on impressionable coeds by mischievous male students. No matter what the source of the haunting, tales of this most famous of all ETSU ghosts have survived, earning a secure place in campus folklore in spite of the odd twist that research has brought to the story in recent years.

The ghost was said to be a very unhappy, very beautiful young woman, the daughter of George L. Carter, the philanthropist who donated the land on which ETSU was built. Alice, as the students called her, was said to have fallen in love with a young man. Both intended marriage, but the young man was poor, and Alice's wealthy father refused permission for his daughter to marry. In a fit of despondency, Alice saw no further point in living and ingested a lethal dose of rat poison.

Carter was grief-stricken at the loss of his only child. He immortalized the image of his lovely daughter in a stained-glass window he installed in the family's house. It was a memorial to her innocence and beauty. The modest window, about twelve by eighteen inches, was a beautiful specimen of leaded glass.

When George Carter died in 1936, the college purchased the house and eighteen acres of land for thirty-five thousand dollars. Ten years later, the college renamed the house Cooper Hall and opened it as a dormitory for senior women. It was then that the haunting began. A female voice was heard singing in the halls. There were unearthly screams. Objects moved from their resting places or disappeared completely, only to reappear unexpectedly much later. Some of the girls experienced the eerie feeling that someone or something was peering over their shoulders. Of course, when they turned around, no one was there. Most of these supernatural events occurred in the vicinity of the stained-glass window, which was located

at the head of a grand staircase. When the house was finally abandoned, the window became a target for vandals. University officials
ordered it removed. Since that time, it has been lost.

Writer Marianne Pearson visited the abandoned building before
the stained-glass window was removed. At the time, she was a student at East Tennessee State and was preparing a Halloween story
for the campus newspaper, the *East Tennessean*. Accompanied by
friends, she entered the building and immediately experienced a
sense of foreboding. The group visited the upper floors of the house,
then descended the creaky stairs and inspected the basement, where
Alice was said to have taken her life. After an initial tour of the
house, they settled in for the night.

Writing years later in the *Elizabethton Star*, Pearson explained how
odd and unexplained things began to happen at that point: "We were
talking about the house and began to hear noises. Pipes clanked in
the basement, but if any member of the group started toward the
stairs to investigate, the beating stopped. Invisible feet walked about
over our heads on the second floor, despite there was no one else in
the house. An electric range's burner was glowing red-hot in the
kitchen . . . when no one had touched the controls. And when I was
speaking, others in the group said the pipes would begin to rattle
again, although I could not hear them. We returned to the basement
and found that when another girl entered the room where the main
water lines were, the pipes began to rattle. Touching the pipes, one
young man discovered that one end of the largest water line was icy
cold, while the other was hot. There was no water in either end, and
no cut-off valve between the two areas. At 1 A.M., the spirit's favorite
hour to make her presence known, we gathered beneath the stained
glass window to await her appearance or some manifestation of her
arrival. None came. Finally at 4 A.M., we packed up our cameras,
blankets and flashlights and left the premises."

When Johnson City historian Ray Stahl began looking into the
Cooper Hall haunting, he made a startling discovery. George Carter
had no daughter! Instead, Carter and his wife, Mayetta, had one
son, James "Jimmy" Walter Carter. Judging by his photographs,
Jimmy was a beautiful child, with long and flowing hair as pretty as

any girl's. Though he was his parents' pride and joy, they were nevertheless disappointed because they were unable to parent a girl.

Stahl argues that Jimmy was used as the artist's model for the stained-glass window. He believes that the figure in the window in Cooper Hall was that of an imaginary daughter that the Carters wished they had, combined with the face of the son they actually did parent!

It is open to debate whether the ghost of Alice was just a figment of someone's vivid imagination. According to some of the older maintenance personnel at ETSU—those who spend time alone at night in the university buildings—the janitorial staff was well aware of the strange goings-on in Cooper Hall. Some even had experiences with the ghost.

After Cooper Hall ceased to be used as a dormitory, the building was utilized as office space. The attic housed the campus FM radio station. Some of the ghostly activity at that time came from the attic. According to one janitor, music would suddenly be heard from the radio station in the middle of the night. One time, the janitor climbed to the attic to investigate and found a record playing on the turntable. No one else was in the building at the time.

Just before Cooper Hall was demolished in 1984, university officials said that the reason for the razing was that the old building would cost too much to renovate. Furthermore, they pointed out that Cooper Annex, as the building was then called, had became an inviting target for vandals and trespassers, and that the university was afraid someone would get hurt in the building.

But some of the janitorial staff employed by the university in the early 1980s suspect there was another reason—the real reason—why Cooper Annex was demolished. According to them, the university could not find anyone brave enough to clean Cooper Annex at night, the time when the ghost walked.

Motifs: E 338. Non-malevolent ghost haunts building; E 338.7.* Ghost haunts educational institution; E 339.1. Non-malevolent ghost haunts spot of former activity or spot for which he has affection; E 338.1(hb). Ghost cleans house; E 402. Mysterious ghostlike sounds are heard; E 328.* Dead returns for something forgotten; E 419.10. Concern of ghost about belongings of his lifetime; E 402.1.2(a). Ghostly footsteps follow living person in house; E 531(c). Person hears part of building fall, finds that nothing has fallen; E 281.3. Ghost haunts particular room in house; E 402.1.1.2. Ghost moans; E 532. Ghostlike picture; E 402.1.1.3. Ghost cries and screams; E 402.1.1.4. Ghost sings; E 599.6. Ghost moves furniture and household articles; E 275. Ghost haunts place of great accident or misfortune; E 334.2.3(b). Ghost of young woman who dies as tragic lover; E 3338.2(b). Ghost appears in church window.

THE
FACE IN
THE FOG

One foggy night in 1922, there occurred a double tragedy near the old waterfront in Kingsport—two automobile accidents that gave birth to one of the best-known upper East Tennessee ghost legends. It is a tale of amazing coincidence. The double tragedy yielded two ghosts—that of a man killed in a freak accident, and that of the automobile that killed him.

"Well, Ol' Hugh is out again tonight," workers arriving for the graveyard shift at Tennessee Eastman often tell employees just leaving after the second shift. "Better listen to him. He says the fog's pretty thick and dangerous out there."

After driving the Netherland Inn Road on foggy nights, many of those workers on the graveyard shift at Tennessee Eastman's sprawling plant have already seen Hugh Hamblen's familiar form—a long trench coat draped over his broad shoulders, his head crowned with a wide-brimmed, outdated hat. He stands silently in the swirling mist, waving caution to drivers feeling their way through the thick fog. The workers at Tennessee Eastman are quite correct. Ol' Hugh warns drivers to be careful. He is such a regular sight near the old waterfront that many motorists are not startled by his appearance. In fact, some drivers and their passengers wave back to him in greeting. Hugh Hamblen is an expert on the dangers of the fog, for he was killed in the fog over sixty years ago. Ol' Hugh is not only the most-seen ghost in upper East Tennessee, but probably also the most helpful.

The story began when Hugh's son, Charlie, was out joyriding with a group of five friends one night near Kingsport. Charlie and the other boys had enjoyed a night of partying, drinking, and carousing. By the time they decided to head for home, the entire pack had overindulged in booze and merrymaking.

Rain had fallen earlier in the evening. Fog was beginning to rise from the valleys, and a thick mist hugged the road. Visibility was nearly zero in some of the low spots. Since the road runs parallel to the Holston River, that made the fog worse. As the Ford touring car the boys were riding in neared Rotherwood Bridge, spanning the Holston on Rogersville Pike, a dog suddenly ran across the road. The car swerved, skidded, and smacked into the bridge with the heart-stopping sound of shattering glass and crumpling metal. Two boys were killed outright, another was fatally injured, and Charlie Hamblen and the remaining two were seriously hurt.

The injured were taken to Kingsport Hospital, which was located directly behind the Netherland Inn at that time. Hugh Hamblen was roused from a sound sleep by the ringing of his telephone and told of his son's accident. He slipped on his clothes and hurried to the hospital. He found that the boy was alive. Hamblen and his son were very close, and Hugh remained at the hospital until early morning.

All night long, Charlie's condition steadily improved. He had suffered internal injuries and a slight concussion. As the shock of the accident began to wear off, his vital signs were returning to normal, and he was much calmer than he had been earlier. When his son drifted off into a drug-induced sleep, Hugh watched him carefully to make certain that his breathing was regular. When word came to him that another of the boys had died of his injuries, he whispered a prayer of thanksgiving that his son's life had been spared. Satisfied that Charlie was out of danger, Hugh finally decided to go home. He stood up, took one last worried look at his son, then passed through the door.

The fog that had begun to swirl into Kingsport earlier in the evening had thickened dramatically. According to the *Bristol Herald-Courier*, Hugh had just left the hospital and walked across the street when a Ford driven by a woman "got out from under control" and ran him down, knocking him over a twenty-foot embankment and then falling on top of him and crushing him. Hugh was pulled from under the wreckage barely alive and carried across Rogersville Pike to the hospital. At the same moment he died, his injured son began to bleed profusely from the ears.

Charlie Hamblen never recovered from the sudden death of his father, nor did he ever completely shake the notion that he was at least partially responsible for the tragedy. Charlie was released from the hospital in time for his father's burial three days later in Kingsport. After that, many people say, Charlie's personality changed. He was no longer fun-loving and outgoing.

A few years later, during an especially dense fog near the old Kingsport waterfront, the ghost of Hugh Hamblen was seen for the first time. At first, motorists believed the form standing on the road and waving for motorists to slow down was a drunken bum who had been disoriented by the fog. Then, as the story goes, the form stepped in front of an auto whose driver saw him too late. There was a squeal of brakes, but the car failed to stop in time. The car appeared to have hit the man, but a search failed to find a body. The "victim" had totally disappeared.

When authorities turned to question the driver of the car that had hit the man, he, too, had disappeared—driven off. Then someone said he thought the driver might have been Charlie Hamblen. Since that night, whenever fog shrouds the old waterfront, the ghost of Hugh Hamblen has been seen by motorists.

A professor at East Tennessee State University had an interesting experience with the ghost several years ago. The professor was determined that he was going to see the ghost of Ol' Hugh, so he began to drive up and down the Netherland Inn Road every night in hopes of finding the ghost. One night, he spied an antique Ford lying on its side in the middle of the road. At first, he believed that there had been an accident, but when he stopped his car and got out, he suddenly realized that the car wasn't really there. He approached the apparition and passed his hand through it several times. Then he turned and walked back to his vehicle. When he switched on the lights of his car, the phantom Ford was still there. Then he started his car, shifted into drive, and drove right through the apparition.

Instead of seeing Ol' Hugh, the professor had encountered the apparition of the car that had killed him. He still drives the Netherland Inn Road, anxious to see the shade of Hugh Hamblen, but so far his only brush with the famous ghost has been a vision of a phantom car.

Motifs: E 422.4.5(b). Male revenant in old-fashioned garb; E 363. Ghost returns to aid living [also E 363.2(c). Ghost prevents automobile accident; E 363.2(e). Ghost guides traveler lost in fog]; E 332.2.2. Ghost of person killed in accident seen at death or burial spot; E 535. Ghostlike conveyance [cf. E 535.4(c). Phantom train reenacts wreck].

THE
HOUSE OF THE
MYSTERIOUS
LIGHT

On Greenwood Drive in Johnson City stands a ramshackle old house suffering a terminal case of neglect. The structure is abandoned, its wooden siding weathered to a nondescript gray. It looks as if it might collapse into a heap of splinters at any moment. Its front, sides, and back are matted with tangled undergrowth.

The house contains an eerie ghost light that occasionally emerges through a side door, travels across Greenwood Drive, and suddenly blinks out in the middle of the road. No one knew the origin of the ghost light for many years, until one night the mystery was dramatically solved by an eyewitness who suddenly remembered a half-forgotten bit of family lore from his home in Rogersville.

The house was probably built before the turn of the century. Little was known of the person who lived there. Old-timers in the area heard, from their fathers and grandfathers, that the house was built by an old man who kept mostly to himself. Legend had it that when the old man died, the house was never lived in again. Once abandoned, it promptly fell into ruin.

One night in the 1930s, a man named McCarney was walking home from work when he saw a glow he took to be a lantern appear from inside the house, emerge through a side door, and begin moving across the road. Wondering who was in the house, and not having heard the story of the ghost light, he called to the person he believed to be carrying the lantern. The light suddenly disappeared. Thinking the carrier had fallen and dropped the lantern, he ran to help, but he could find neither the lantern nor its bearer. Then, as he turned toward the house, the light again appeared at the window, emerged through the door, and came toward him. When it was about fifteen feet away, it stopped. McCarney peered into the darkness at the ghostly glow. There was no person in sight. Then the light winked out. Panicked, McCarney turned and ran all the way home, not stopping until he was safely behind his own door.

The next day, he told a friend what had happened. His friend did not believe him immediately, but his curiosity was aroused. The two agreed to return to the house that night. By eight o'clock, they were hidden in some bushes along the side of the road. After two hours, a yellow glow appeared in one of the first-floor windows.

"See!" McCarney hissed to his friend. "I told you." Then he started to cross the road.

"Wait," his friend cautioned. "Let's see what happens next."

Slowly, the light drifted through the first floor of the house. Then it moved outside and onto the road, swinging as if someone were carrying it. The two men held their breath. The light was moving across the road, in their direction. A blood-curdling scream shattered the stillness, and then the light winked out. There was not a living soul to be seen. The two men stared at each other in astonishment.

"Did you hear a scream last night?" the shaken friend asked McCarney.

"No," McCarney replied. "There was the light and nothing else."

The two men then adjourned to McCarney's house for some much-needed liquid refreshment.

The next day, intrigued by what they had seen and heard, they returned to the house and peered into the windows. Sunlight played on the bare walls and the plain wooden floors. Nothing seemed the least bit unusual. The two decided to return to the house later that night with additional witnesses.

About ten o'clock, the light again appeared at the window. This time, a half-dozen men crouched in the bushes on the other side of the road. The yellow glow slowly moved through the house, as if the lantern were being carried by someone who was old and feeble. Finally, the glow emerged through the door and began moving across the road. McCarney squinted into the darkness, trying to see what was carrying the lantern. There was a dark shape, but its features were indistinguishable. When the glow reached the center of the road, a scream rent the air and the light winked out.

"Oh my God!" one of the men hidden in the bushes cried. "That was my grandfather!"

The others, shaken, turned to him and asked him what he meant.

"In our family, there's a story about my grandfather, who left my grandmother shortly after my father was born," he said. "That was around Rogersville. No one ever heard from him again, but it was said that he came to Johnson City and worked for a time as a rigger at Jobe's Opera House."

"Doesn't anyone know what happened to him?" one of the men asked.

"I don't think that anyone really cared," the man replied. "He was a very mean-minded person, and most people thought it was good riddance that he was gone. My grandmother married again years later, and I don't think she ever tried to find him."

"But how could the light have anything to do with your grand-father?" another man asked.

Just then, the ghost light reappeared in the first floor of the house. The man telling the story said, "Watch when the light comes out again. Watch the way it swings. My grandfather's right leg was about three inches shorter than the other, I believe from the effects of polio when he was a kid."

The light passed through the door and started to cross the road. The man continued, "When the light swings, it suddenly drops down like whoever is holding it loses his footing for a second. Watch."

The light swung slowly across the road and, sure enough, the arc in which it swung was not smooth, as it should have been. Every second or two, it would suddenly dip. No one had noticed that before. When it reached the center of the road, there was a feeble scream, not as loud and clear as the first time, and the light disappeared.

Once again, the men were a bit shaken. "But I still don't understand what the light has to do with your grandfather," one of them said.

"It's simple," the man answered. "About fifteen or twenty years after he left my grandmother, we heard he'd been killed. He walked from his house one night, a lantern in his hand, and was run over by a wagon. This house must have been where he lived all those years after he ran off. Of course, I can't prove it for sure, but I'd bet a week's pay that's the ghost of my grandfather out there."

Just then, the ghost light began to cross the road for the third time that night. The whole tragic accident appeared to be in perpetual replay, but now the story was clear. Though the ghost holding the light was invisible, and though the man had never met his grandfather, he had solved the mystery on the strength of an old family story alone, with the ghost's limp and the scream as the principal clues.

"I don't wish hell on anybody," the man said. "But if the stories I heard about my grandfather are true, nobody ever deserved this more than he did."

Motifs: E 599.7. Ghost carries lantern; E 530.1. Ghostlike lights; E 402. Mysterious ghostlike noises heard; E 334. Non-malevolent ghost haunts scene of former misfortune, crime, or tragedy; #338. Non-malevolent ghost haunts building.

THE
WITCH'S
WRATH

There are plenty of stories about witches in upper East Tennessee. In those areas farthest removed from cities and towns, belief in witches is strongest. One such antisocial miscreant has been torturing a Carter County farmer for many years. The man wants only to live in peace, but he incurred the wrath of a woman he believes holds power not only over his farm and livestock, but also over his life.

It all began when the woman's three children started playing in an abandoned, rickety barn on the farmer's land. Fearful for the safety of the children, he tried at first to reason with them, then finally had to chase them away. The children returned repeatedly, and the exasperated farmer spoke to their mother. She assured him that she would order her children to stay away from the dangerous barn.

The children—about seven, eight, and ten years old—were not the sort to obey anyone, not even their mother. Nor were they going to stay out of a structure that offered so much potential for adventure and fun. After a week, the farmer visited the mother again and asked her to talk to her offspring. This time, the woman became abusive, claiming that the farmer was harassing her children for no reason.

"They ain't hurtin' nothin'!" she screamed. "Why don't you leave them alone?" The woman seemed so out of control that the farmer was dumbfounded.

Soon after the confrontation, the woman's middle child, a boy, fell through the rotten hayloft floor and as a result of his injuries was paralyzed from the waist down. The farmer feared he would be sued. He visited the woman and expressed his sympathies, but reiterated that she and her offspring had been warned repeatedly what might happen if the children continued to play in the barn.

The mother screwed up her nose, and her eyes suddenly became steely. "You tried to kill my little boy," she hissed at the surprised farmer. "You booby-trapped that place, and now he can't walk. You nearly killed him! Now he's ruined for life!"

Then she casually announced that she was a witch and would "fix" him for hurting one of her children. No denial on the farmer's part would convince the woman otherwise. He left the woman's house thinking she would eventually cool down and he would try to talk to her again. It was not her claim of witchcraft that worried him, but the possibility of an expensive lawsuit.

A day or two later, the farmer's house mysteriously caught fire, but the blaze was extinguished before the flames caused much damage. A week later, the farmer's wife went to the chicken house to collect eggs and found, to her horror, that all of her prize layers had been slaughtered and their blood smeared on the walls. That same evening, two of the farmer's best mules keeled over dead, for no apparent reason. The next morning, his blue tick hound was found in the front yard torn limb from limb.

The farmer contacted the local authorities and reported the slaughter of his animals. Then he told them of the woman and her child, her accusations against him, and the fact that she claimed she was a witch.

"Do you really think she might be a witch?" the sheriff asked.

"How else would you explain what's been happening to me?" the frightened farmer asked in return.

The authorities dutifully visited the woman's house to question her. The fact that the farmer was convinced she was a witch did little for his credibility. The woman, on the other hand, appeared rather saintly in the care of her crippled child. The authorities found the other children well-behaved and mannerly. They were clearly not the rowdy urchins that the farmer had described. Furthermore, the woman didn't even look like a witch. While not a young woman, neither was she an old crone. Her appearance was pleasant and her voice almost lilting. And she even offered the sheriff's deputies fresh-brewed coffee and homemade sugar cookies.

The authorities returned and told the farmer that unless he could show them hard evidence to the contrary, they would not arrest the woman. "This is not Salem," the sheriff told him. "The law doesn't prosecute witches anymore. Now, did you see anyone suspicious hanging around your farm before your animals died or your house caught fire?" From that moment, the investigation centered on the possibility that the damage to the house and the death of the animals had been caused by youthful vandals.

As the weeks passed, one head after another of the farmer's live-stock died. As soon as a pig or a cow was replaced, another was lost. The farmer was convinced that his neighbor was at the bottom of his troubles. And animal deaths were not the only misfortune he suffered. A creek that ran through his property suddenly dried up, for no apparent reason. Then his well became tainted, and he was forced to dig another. His wife grew ill and was laid up many weeks.

A year passed. The sheriff's office was stymied over the death of the farmer's animals, and the investigation had ground to a halt. In the meantime, the farmer's misfortunes continued—more livestock died, and a third well had to be dug to replace the second, which had also become tainted. Finally, the farmer could take no more misfor-tune. He began entertaining thoughts of a desperate measure.

One night, he walked to the woman's house, a .38 Special tucked into his belt with six deadly shells in the chamber. It was very dark—no moon or stars—and very silent. For five minutes, he stood out-side her lighted window, periodically taking a swig from a whiskey bottle and trying to summon up the courage to commit murder.

The woman was seated at her kitchen table, her back toward him, apparently unaware of his presence. Everything looked normal inside the house. It was late, and her children had already gone to bed. The farmer knew he would not find a better opportunity.

He cocked his pistol and pointed it through the window, taking aim at the back of the woman's head. He knew that what he was doing was terribly wrong. The sheriff would not have much trouble determining who had committed the crime. Yet didn't the Bible say, "Thou shalt not suffer a witch to live"?

His hand trembled as serious doubts raced through his head. What if he were wrong about her? He lowered the gun slightly, then raised it back up. He had been threatened by her, then all sorts of mysterious things had begun happening to him. She had to be the reason! She had to be a witch, just like she claimed.

His finger squeezed slightly on the trigger. Then, without warning, the woman turned—not her body, just her head, a full 180 degrees. She stared directly at him, her eyes flashing with the fire of satisfaction. The terrified farmer dropped his pistol, ran all the way home, burst into the house, and locked the door behind him.

Then, two weeks later, for some unexplained reason, the woman's paralyzed youngster gained his legs. The woman claimed that the cure was a miracle of God, but the farmer knew better.

He has seldom seen the woman since the night he pointed a pistol at her, and no further misfortune has befallen him—at least not the kind that he can blame on the doings of a witch. The woman apparently had all the vengeance she needed. But the farmer still lives in fear. And he is not totally convinced that his troubles won't start again, even if he continues to give his magical neighbor a wide berth.

Motifs: G 260. Evil deeds of witches; G 269.10. Witch punishes person who incurs her ill will. D 2080.* Bewitching by ill-wishing; G 265. Witch abuses property; D 2080. Magic against property; G 265.4.0.1. Witch punishes owner for injury or slight by killing his animals; D 2151. Magical control of waters; G 263.4. Witch causes illness; D 2064. Magical sickness [cf. D 269.4.(b). Witch curses person who injures or insults her; the person becomes ill]; D 2137. Natural law suspended; D 2161. Magic healing power.

THE
AMAZING
LENA JONES

Researchers say the human mind is an untapped well of incredible and unexplained power. Some people are able to tap a portion of that hidden force locked in their heads. There are some people, for example, who claim they can accurately tell the future, see clearly into the past, and even see ghosts when the notion strikes them. Such people are called psychics or intuitives.

One of the best known of all upper East Tennessee intuitives was Lena Jones of Bristol. She was said to be able to see into the future and the past, find lost objects, and tell not only what kind of ghost haunted a house, but who that particular ghost was.

"Miracles happen for me all the time," she said. "I live completely by faith, because that's all I got—faith and a little ol' Social Security check."

A diminutive, grandmotherly woman, Lena had a friendly face and clear blue eyes offset by a little bow of a mouth that was constantly upturned in a smile. She possessed her unique ability from the time she was young, although she didn't recognize it as anything special until quite late in life.

"The first things I remember seeing were wreaths hanging on

doors," she said. "And then somebody would die in the house. I remember I once saw a wreath hanging on a door across the street. I ran into the house to tell my mama that somebody was dead in that house. And she said, 'Nobody's dead over there. And don't lie like that or I'll spank you.' And I said, 'I saw a wreath hanging on the door.' And the next day, somebody did die in that house—I think with a heart attack—and the next day there was a wreath hanging on the door."

Her mother must have told everyone that Lena had seen a wreath on the door, because later several neighbors gathered on the street corner and motioned for Lena to come to them.

"I assumed everyone could see things," Lena said. "I didn't know that they couldn't. The neighbors asked me questions about themselves and their families—things that had happened to them in the past—and I would answer. And the neighbors would look at each other, smile, and nod their heads." She chuckled when she added, "I must've told them right, I guess."

As Lena grew into womanhood, her abilities became more widely known. One day, she visited the historic Netherland Inn in Kingsport and astounded witnesses with the powers she displayed. Though she knew absolutely nothing of the inn's history, she accurately described a number of events that had occurred there.

She also visited the Deery Inn, which had been the site of a makeshift hospital during the Battle of Blountville in the Civil War. Without any prior knowledge of events at the inn, she discovered that during the battle the wounded were laid outside on blankets and coverlets, babies were placed in a corner of the building, and the crippled and infirm were placed in separate sections outside the structure. Very few people were aware of such details, but Lena knew them just by looking around the old grounds.

Because of her uncanny powers, Lena was often used by police departments to help track down criminals or to find stolen property. On occasion, she was also called on to solve the mystery of houses alleged to be haunted. She demonstrated her abilities once when she was invited to Jonesborough to tour the town in search of haunted buildings. She spent nearly a day in town, visited a number of the older homes, and told residents things that had occurred there.

In the former Blue Iris Tea Room, located in a large white building on a hill overlooking Jonesborough, she found a room in which she suddenly became unreasonably cold. For a moment, she could not understand her feeling. Then she said that two people had died of consumption in the room. Subsequent investigation proved she was right. The former owners of the house had lost two children to tuberculosis.

At another location, Lena was inexplicably drawn to a storehouse located at the rear of an apartment. When she opened the door, she understood why she had felt an urge to enter the room and why she had felt such a sense of foreboding. On the far wall, there was scrawled a huge, faded pentagram—an ancient and infamous symbol of witchcraft. The room had been a former meeting place for Satanists.

So it was as she traveled through Jonesborough, constantly followed by a crowd of interested onlookers, television camera operators, and news reporters. In one home, the owners had for many years felt an unknown, ominous presence. There were no ghosts or other indications that had led them to believe that their home was haunted, just a feeling of oppression that occasionally enveloped the house, especially late at night, when it was quiet. Lena was not told of this when she entered the house for a reception held in her honor at the end of her day in Jonesborough. Suddenly, she turned to one of the owners and asked him to take her upstairs. When they returned, the owner was visibly shaken. Lena had discovered that two children had died of diphtheria in an upstairs bedroom, and that their spirits were still in the house.

One stop on Lena's tour of Jonesborough surprised local residents. The ancient town cemetery contains the remains of almost a hundred victims of a cholera epidemic, but it failed to elicit any response from Lena. "Ghosts are not always in places where you would expect them," she told the expectant crowd. "In fact, cemeteries are the least haunted places in the world. When a person dies, their body is just clay. The spirit is gone somewhere else—the spirit is not there."

Lena was not always so matter-of-fact about her powers. "I had been married and had a divorce when I found out that everybody couldn't see the things that I did, and it scared me," she said. "I thought, who am I? What am I?"

Some people were afraid, and treated her like a freak of nature. But gradually, Lena accepted her special gift and determined to use it to help people. She never accepted any money for the work she did for others.

Eventually, she came to believe that her powers were from God. "I had been raised in a church," she said, "but I don't believe in the churches anymore, because denomination means division. We are the church, ourselves. And God is within us. And God is a spirit. And we're a part of it. We're part of the whole. And the spirit knows all things. And the more in the spirit you are, the more you can see."

Lena said that she prayed all the time—that she had to pray to live. One day, one of her prayers was answered in a most startling way. "An apple tree stood at the foot of my steps, and I had my clothesline tied to it," she said. "And there were little, hard apples on this tree, and they'd fall on the ground and rot under the tree. And the bees would swarm underneath there. I got stung seven times in one day while hanging up clothes."

She asked her landlady for permission to cut down the tree, but the woman refused because it provided the only shade for one of the upstairs apartments. "So I said to myself, 'That's okay, I'll pray it down,'" Lena remembered.

"I was hanging out clothes that morning and this neighbor—she had the other apartment across the yard—was sitting on her steps. Her little girl was playing around my clothesline, and I was afraid that she would be stung by the bees. And I told my neighbor, 'You know, the Bible says that you can say to yon tree, "Be plucked up and be cast into the sea."' And after I had finished hanging my clothes on the clothesline, I just held my hand up and I said, 'God, move this tree.'"

By five o'clock that afternoon, Lena had gathered her clothes from the clothesline and laid them carefully on the bed. Suddenly, she felt God come into the house. "And He was here!" she said. "And I knew He was here! And nobody heard the tree fall, but my daughter was in the kitchen and she said, 'Mama, this tree is a-lyin' on the ground.'"

The tree had fallen away from the house. It had not split above the ground. It was as if some giant hand had reached down and ripped it from the earth, roots and all. Then the neighbor she had been talking to earlier in the day ran up excitedly and said, "Mrs. Jones, your prayer's answered. This tree's a-lyin' on the ground!"

Scientists and researchers will continue trying to unlock the unexplained powers of the human mind for many years to come. They would do well to pay close attention to the accounts of a little, grandmotherly woman from Bristol who demonstrated an ability to find lost objects, to identify ghosts, to see into the past and the future—even to pray down an apple tree.

Motifs: D 1825.1. Second sight, power to see future happenings; D 1825.7. Magic sight of incident before it actually happens; D 2080. Magic used against property; D 176.6.7.1. Magic results produced in name of deity; G 265.10. Witches bewitch trees; G 265.10.2. Witches kill plants.

THE
BACKFIRING OF
BLACK AGGIE

Nearly every graveyard has its "Black Aggie" story. Black Aggie is the generic name for a horrifying apparition said to lurk in the shadows of tombstones late at night, often during episodes of dense fog or when the moon is full, waiting to leap out and snatch away a living victim, usually a woman.

Black Aggie stories vary little from location to location. The Black Aggie is usually described as a hag with flaming red eyes, dressed all in black, having a skeletal face and emitting a horrific scream. The apparition is usually identified as the ghost of a woman—often suspected of having been a witch while she was alive—who died alone and miserable because people were afraid of her. Her haunting of a particular graveyard, in which she may or may not actually be buried, is said to be her way to wreak vengeance on the living. She is said to be in league with the devil, promoted from witch to the exalted rank of demon after her death, possessing even more infernal power than she had while alive.

The authenticity of most Black Aggie stories is highly suspect. Boys—especially teenage boys—like to make up such stories to terrify their girlfriends. The ghost lore of upper East Tennessee is rife with Black Aggie stories, most of them fake.

One October in Greeneville in the early 1960s, a certain young man and several of his friends decided they would play a prank on one of their female schoolmates. Not only was the girl very pretty, but she seemed to be quite gullible and game for any new adventure— a prime candidate for some well-planned ghostly activity.

The young man began the gag by informing the girl that on Halloween, a ghost often appeared over a certain tombstone in a cemetery located just off what is now U.S. 11E. Then he told her that he and some of his friends were going to visit the cemetery to see the ghost. Of course, she wanted to be included in the party.

What the girl did not know was that the young man and his friends were arranging for their own phantom to appear, an apparition that would pop from behind the tombstone on cue and scare the girl out of seven years' growth. One of the boys had devised a serviceable costume made from filmy cheesecloth, complete with a rubber fright mask that he had bought in a big-city novelty store.

At the appointed hour on Halloween, everyone met in the graveyard. Suddenly, the girl was not as brave as she had been earlier, and the young man had to keep her from running away. The closer they came to the tombstone, the more she resisted, and by the time they were a few feet away, the boys were literally pulling her along with them.

Right on cue, the "phantom" popped up from behind the tombstone, and the girl screamed and fainted. The boys were laughing so hard that they hardly noticed that the phantom was moving away from them and heading toward the woods.

When the young man who had organized the prank was through congratulating himself, he called to his friend, the phantom. But the friend did not reappear. Then one of the boys looked behind the tombstone and discovered that the boy in the costume was still there—lying on the ground, passed out cold.

As soon as he revived, he told his story. He had been crouched in the dark behind the tombstone, ready to spring, when a face suddenly appeared in front of him. It snarled, and that was the last thing that he remembered.

Then one of the boys yelled out a warning. The phantom was returning from the woods, heading directly toward them. It was a real Black Aggie! The boys scrambled to their feet, yelling at the top of their lungs, and hightailed it out of the graveyard, leaving the still passed-out girl to fend for herself.

The next day, the girl was mad as a scorned lover. "Why did you leave me in that place?" she asked the young man who had invited her, when she saw him in the hallway at school.

He confessed about the practical joke and told her what had really happened. He said he was sorry and that he had not believed there was really a ghost in the cemetery. He said that when they saw the Black Aggie coming towards them, they had forgotten about everything but their own skins.

The girl looked thoughtful for a minute, then asked, "You mean to tell me there was a real ghost in that graveyard?"

"Yes," he replied meekly. "There really was."

"I don't believe you," she answered.

"But you were so frightened that you fainted," he protested.

"Not at your silly ghost. Luckily, mine had a car."

By now, the young man was thoroughly confused, so the girl suggested that he turn around and look behind him. Standing in the hallway was the same "apparition" that he had seen the night before, the one that had made his friend in the costume faint. The ghost removed its mask, revealing the pretty face of another of his female classmates.

"I just thought that if your Black Aggie didn't show up, I'd bring my own along just in case," the girl said, laughing. "I would have really hated to disappoint you!"

Motifs: H 1410. Fear test: staying in frightful place; K 1682.1. "Big 'Fraid and Little 'Fraid": trickster disguised as ghost attempts to scare others, is scared himself; cf. E 236.3(c). Boys raise ghost as a lark, are scared by the ghost; K 1600. Deceiver falls into own traps; K 1699(1).* Boys arrange for sexton to scare girlfriends in cemetery. Girls run, take care; boys must walk back to town.

PART OF THE DARK IS MOVING: THE HAUNTED BRIDGE AT STONY CREEK

The section of the Watauga River near the community of Stony Creek is brush-tangled and spooky. After dark, long shadows reach across the river, creating fantastic shapes.

A creaking steel-girder bridge built in the late 1920s spans the river on the road between Elizabethton and Watauga Lake. When the bridge was new, the people of Stony Creek looked upon it proudly as a welcome addition to the community.

It wasn't long before the secluded area beneath the bridge became notorious as a place for lovers to find a bit of nocturnal privacy. One night in the early 1930s, a local rake and his girlfriend of the moment found a comfortable place to settle underneath the bridge. Tom Jackson was the son of a successful Elizabethton businessman. His companion, Wanda Smithson, was the daughter of a Carter County truck farmer.

The two had been keeping company for several weeks and had used the bridge several times before as a sanctuary. On previous occasions, they had found the area beneath the bridge crowded with couples. But this night, Tom and Wanda were lucky. Even though the evening was clear and warm, and a Friday night to boot, they found themselves alone. Wanda had been nervous when others were around, because she feared they would recognize her and go tell her father what they had seen. Her father had a puritanical streak and would no doubt punish her. So for the first time, she was able to relax and enjoy Tom's embraces.

About ten o'clock, Wanda suggested that they had better head for home before their passions got out of hand. Tom reluctantly agreed. As the couple rose to leave, they noticed a figure scrambling down the bank toward them. At first, they assumed another pair of lovers was arriving, but they became uneasy when a second person did not appear. Suddenly, the figure, a huge man, made a dash for them, and Tom caught a momentary glint of shiny steel as a knife plunged deeply into Wanda's chest. She gasped, her face contorting in pain. Another glint and the knife once again struck Wanda. She fell back against the bank dead.

The man turned to Tom, his knife raised in the air, poised to strike a third time. As Tom turned to run, he felt excruciating pain as the knife ripped into his back. Then he felt a searing flash in his chest, and blood exploded from his mouth. Every breath suddenly became a chore, but somehow he made it to the top of the bank. His assailant was after him, scrambling over loose rocks and dirt, wildly slashing the air with his knife.

On the west end of the bridge, a Ford touring car was just beginning to cross. Nearly blind from intense pain, Tom could just see the fuzzy glow of the car's headlights. With the murderer's footsteps behind him, he made a mad dash across the bridge, reached the car, tore open the back door, and leaped into the seat, landing heavily in the lap of a smartly dressed woman. The woman screamed. The driver of the car, seeing the man with the knife poised above his head, ready to strike, stepped on the gas and sped off the bridge. It was only a moment later that he realized that someone had jumped into the back seat of his car, and that it was not the man with the knife who had made his passenger scream.

"Wanda's dead," Tom croaked in as loud a voice as his slashed lungs would allow. "And I'm sure kilt."

He was rushed to the hospital. He died an hour later, but not before he coughed out his story to the police. The authorities combed the area beneath and surrounding the bridge but found neither a sign of the knife-wielding man nor the body of Wanda Smithson. Strangely, no blood from the murdered girl was found under the bridge. No convincing explanation for the disappearance of Wanda's body or the lack of bloodstains has ever been offered.

At first, residents of Stony Creek were nervous that the murderer was still at large in their community. But as the months passed and there were no further incidents, the fear finally subsided.

A short time after the double murder, the first incident of ghostly activity on the bridge was reported. Another followed, and a legend began to grow. Witnesses claimed there was a ghost that jumped into the back seat of passing automobiles. Those in the car would hear the sound of a back door slamming and notice a sudden depression of the back seat—like someone had sat down. People who have experienced the haunting firsthand say the physical sensation is startling. Local tradition says it is the ghost of Tom Jackson trying to get help for himself and his girlfriend. However, no one has ever actually seen the ghost, so its true identity remains uncertain.

In the late 1960s, five students from a beauty school in Knoxville were on their way to Watauga Lake. The women had heard that if motorists crossed the bridge and failed to lock the back doors, an unseen presence would get into the car. There were other routes to Watauga Lake, but the women, on a lark, decided to cross the bridge.

"If you drive through Stony Creek at twilight, it's spooky," remembered Sharon Messer, one of the passengers in the back seat that night. "There are gnarled trees that lean across little, narrow roads, switchback curves, and all kinds of spooky stuff. It's the way Sleepy Hollow would be, if you can imagine that."

By the time their auto began crossing the bridge, the women were laughing about the ghost. "All of a sudden, I heard the car door open, heard it close, and felt the seat go down beside me," Messer said with a shiver. "The door didn't actually open, but I heard it, and then something invisible sat down on the seat beside me."

She asked the girl sitting beside her, "Did you hear that?"

"Yes," her companion answered in a whisper, "but I was hoping that it was my imagination."

The three women in the front seat must have gotten the message, because the driver pressed on the gas and the car sped across the bridge like the devil himself was after it.

Later, Messer was telling a friend about the experience, and he said that he had a tale of his own to tell about the bridge. The young man had once dated a girl who lived in Stony Creek. Since he had no car at the time, he would walk to her house, then return home late at night, a distance of about a mile. If it was not too late, his father would pick him up and save him the walk.

One night, the young man stayed unusually late at the girl's house. Rather than call his father, he decided to walk home. His route took him across the steel-girder bridge spanning the Watauga River.

As soon as he set foot on the bridge, he heard the sound of footsteps behind him. He turned and looked around. No one was in sight. It was a very dark night, with the moon hidden behind a thick cover of clouds. All that he could see clearly was a glistening in the water beneath the bridge, but there was nothing on the bridge itself. The young man continued his walk. Once again, he heard footsteps behind him.

"He told me that he turned around again," Messer said, "and he saw something move that looked like a darker shadow in the shadows—like part of the dark itself was moving."

A cold shudder traveled up the young man's spine. He walked quickly to the edge of the bridge and ducked into the shadows underneath some low-hanging tree branches. Once again, he stopped and turned. Suddenly, the moon came out from behind the clouds. There, at the end of the bridge, stood a figure that appeared to be wrapped in a monk's robe, a hood covering its head. The face was turned partially away. Then the apparition turned and slowly lifted its head. Underneath the hood was the horrifying face of a skull.

The young man left his hiding place and ran all the way home, his shirttail flapping behind him. He has never dared to cross the haunted bridge again.

Motifs: E 402. Mysterious ghostlike noises are heard; E 332. Non-malevolent road ghosts (cf. E 332.3.3.1. The vanishing hitchhiker; E 581.8.* Ghost rides in automobile); E 421.5. Ghost seen by two or more persons. They corroborate the appearance; E 402. Mysterious ghostlike noises are heard; E 332.1(a). Ghost appears at bridge; E 422.4.5(b). Male revenant in old-fashioned garb; E 422. The living corpse.

"WATCH-GHOST"
OF THE
JOHN SEVIER

When it comes to legend and folklore, tales in the wake of tragedy sprout like weeds in a fallow field. Only a few days after one of the greatest tragedies in the history of Johnson City, there began reports of ghosts haunting an empty building.

On December 24, 1989, a disastrous fire occurred at the John Sevier Center in which sixteen people died, all from smoke inhalation. The building, formerly a hotel, had been renovated and, at the time of the tragedy, was occupied primarily by the elderly and persons on fixed incomes.

The fire began about five o'clock at night on the ground floor, and for the next six hours, the building acted like an eleven-story chimney. Thick, black, acrid smoke billowed up stairwells and into every room through heating ducts, suffocating residents and visitors and making rescue almost impossible. Firefighters wearing heavy smoke-protection gear felt their way through the labyrinth of hallways, entering apartments in search of victims. In the meantime, elderly residents attempted to snake their way down the same smoke-filled halls to street level.

The people of upper East Tennessee watched their television sets solemnly for live on-the-scene reports. Heartrending videotapes were shipped nationwide from a Johnson City television station, and still pictures taken by local newspaper photographers kept satellite transmitting stations busy beaming pictures. By Christmas morning, nearly every newspaper in America, and all major television networks and cable news services, had reported the tragic Christmas Eve fire in Johnson City.

The John Sevier began as a luxury hotel. When it was built in 1924 at a cost of half a million dollars, the original owners advertised that the structure was virtually fireproof. With its magnificent ballroom and fine restaurant, the John Sevier Hotel quickly became the social center of Johnson City. Not even the Great Depression of the 1930s dampened the spirit of the gala dances and receptions held there.

Throughout the 1940s, while still serving as a hotel, the building began to crumble into disrepair. The ballroom, however, retained its popularity. Each Friday night, the dance held there attracted the best of Johnson City society. In the 1950s, the waltzes and polkas were replaced by the driving rhythms of rock music. By then, the patronage at the Friday night dances had changed to teenagers.

In the meantime, businesses were leaving downtown Johnson City for the new malls and business developments of North Roan Street. The grandeur of the John Sevier Hotel faded, and the place became a hangout for vagabonds and prostitutes. Motels on the outskirts of town took most of the remaining legitimate business away from the hotel and, by 1978, owner Marion Palmer was ready to sell. A year later, the building's new owner, businessman Eugene Trivette, remodeled the old hotel into a retirement center and re-named it the John Sevier Center.

It was a decade later that the tragic fire struck. One of the sights that greatly affected firefighters and rescue workers in the early moments of the fire was the appearance of elderly residents at the windows begging to be rescued. One woman appeared in a fourth-floor window, waving feebly to the firefighters arriving below. Another face appeared on the seventh floor, leaning out of a window to avoid inhaling the thick smoke that was boiling from her apartment windows, feebly calling to firefighters.

Three days after the fire, nothing seemed amiss inside the building save the pungent odor of smoke that hung stubbornly in the air. Apartment doors were open, yet it appeared only that the residents had left momentarily on some errand. But the silent halls of the John Sevier Center were not totally empty. The ashes had not yet cooled when apparitions were reported in the building. A number of witnesses saw terrified, ghostly faces of the elderly at the windows of the empty building.

"I was walking up Roan Street about six o'clock one evening, heading for Munsey Church," said an insurance salesman from Jonesborough, "and I happened to look up at the side of the Sevier. In one of the windows, I could clearly see a white-haired old lady—she looked to be in her seventies or eighties—waving as if she were a movie and had been filmed in slow motion. At first, I thought there was someone locked in the building, trying to get out. Then I realized that there could not be any residents in there, because the place was locked up tight. I looked away for some reason, and when I looked again, the woman was gone. My blood ran cold. I knew that I had seen a ghost."

Another witness, a construction worker, saw an apparition inside the building only four days after the fire. On the third floor of the old hotel, he ran into what could only be called a "watch-ghost." In retrospect, the construction worker was grateful to the apparition, because it prevented him from committing a crime that he knew he would regret for the rest of his life.

"It was about four o'clock in the afternoon," the construction worker said. "I had to go up on the third floor to get something or other that they [the workers on the first floor] needed. During the fire, firefighters had confined the flames to the first and second floors, so the third floor was fairly clear of fire damage. Except for the smell of smoke, you could hardly tell anything had happened up there at all.

"Now, everyone else in the building was on the first floor, and I was alone on the third. It was pretty spooky up there. The halls are pretty narrow and close. Some of the doors to the apartments were open, just like the people had left them when they escaped from the hotel. And things in the apartments were pretty much as they had been left. As I said, the fire didn't get up this far—only smoke.

"While looking around, the thing that really got me were all the Xs on the doors. I was told that the Xs were the only way that the firemen could tell if they had searched a room or not during the fire. They'd search a room for victims, and then leave an X on the door to let the next bunch of rescuers know that the room had already been searched, and that all the bodies had been removed from that apartment.

"Well, I ain't very proud of the fact, but I thought that I might go into some of the rooms and see what I could find—maybe some small thing that I could put into my pocket and no one would miss it until it was too late. Well, there I was, and I looked down the hall and I seen this old man standing down there, kind of watching me. He had this walker and he looked pretty feeble. I thought to myself that someone must have wandered in to collect some of his possessions. I knew that some of the residents had been bugging the owners to let them in to get their things, because they were afraid something would get stolen. But the owners were waiting a bit longer. So I thought this guy must have sneaked in past the workmen on the first floor.

"In most of the building, the halls are L-shaped, and this guy turned the corner and walked out of sight. He must have walked down the other side of the hall. I thought that I should go after him and help him out of the building, because it was pretty dangerous in the darkness. I walked down the hallway, turned the corner, and I couldn't see nobody. So I figured that he had gone into one of the rooms. Most of them were unlocked at the time.

"Well, I looked all over the place, and I couldn't find nobody. I searched high and low. So I figured he must have gone down the stairs, but I couldn't figure out how he had moved so fast with that walker. He was kind of feeble, as I said.

"I went back downstairs, and I asked the other guys if they had seen him. No one had, and there were men at all the entrances that were not locked up. I don't know if what I saw was a ghost or not, but that would sure explain how he disappeared so fast."

The construction worker went on to explain that the apparition had looked solid, not transparent or translucent, the way that a ghost would look. After his experience, he had no more thoughts about robbing the empty rooms at the John Sevier Center. He said that every time he thinks about the "watch-ghost," he still gets cold chills.

Motifs: E 275. Ghost haunts place of great accident or misfortune; E 419.10. Concern of ghost about belongings of its lifetime; E 328.* Dead returns for something forgotten; E 334.2.2. Ghost of person killed in accident seen at death or burial spot.